Mediterranean Meals for Two

Quick, Healthy and Delicious Recipes to Share with Your Special Someone

Gabriela Soto

TABLE OF CONTENTS

INTRODUCTION 1

CHAPTER 1: BREAKFAST.. 6

   Classic Omelette 7

   Avocado Toast with Poached Eggs 9

   Pancakes.. 11

   Overnight Chia Pudding 13

   Breakfast Burrito 14

   Yogurt Parfait... 16

   French Toast 17

   Breakfast Quesadillas 18

   Veggie Frittata 20

   Smoothie Bowl.. 22

   Breakfast Tacos 24

   Breakfast Sandwich... 26

   Banana Pancakes 27

   Breakfast Quinoa Bowl 29

   Egg and Veggie Muffin Cups 30

CHAPTER 2: LUNCH RECIPES 32

   Caprese Salad.. 33

   Chickpea Salad Wraps 35

   Quinoa Salad with Roasted Vegetables.. 36

   Mediterranean Hummus Bowl 38

   Avocado Toast 39

   Veggie Wrap 40

   Spinach and Feta Stuffed Bell Peppers 41

   Vegan Buddha Bowl.. 43

   Margherita Panini 44

Lentil and Vegetable Stir-Fry 45

Mexican Quinoa Stuffed Peppers 47

Greek Salad Pita Pockets 49

Vegan Chickpea Curry 51

Caprese Panzanella Salad 53

Veggie Sushi Rolls 54

CHAPTER 3: SOUPS RECIPES **56**

Classic Tomato Soup 57

Butternut Squash Soup 59

Lentil Soup 61

Minestrone Soup 63

Chicken Noodle Soup 65

Potato Leek Soup 67

Creamy Mushroom Soup 69

Tortilla Soup 71

Thai Coconut Curry Soup 73

Broccoli Cheddar Soup 75

Italian Wedding Soup 77

Corn Chowder 79

Black Bean Soup 81

Creamy Cauliflower Soup 83

Moroccan Lentil Soup 85

CHAPTER 4: PIZZA AND PASTA RECIPES **87**

Margherita Pizza 88

Veggie Supreme Pizza 90

BBQ Chicken Pizza 92

Pesto and Tomato Pizza 94

Spinach and Mushroom Pizza 96

Mediterranean Pizza 98

Classic Spaghetti Aglio e Olio 100

Creamy Vegan Alfredo 101

Tomato Basil Pasta 103

Lemon Garlic Pasta 105

Vegan Bolognese 106

Creamy Mushroom Pasta 108

Pesto Pasta 110

Roasted Vegetable Pasta 112

Vegan Carbonara 114

CHAPTER 5: MEAT, POULTRY AND SAFOOD RECIPES **116**

Grilled Steak 117

Baked Lemon Herb Chicken 118

Shrimp Scampi 120

Honey Mustard Glazed Salmon 122

Chicken Fajitas 123

Pan-Seared Pork Chops 125

Lemon Garlic Shrimp Pasta 126

Teriyaki Glazed Chicken Skewers 128

Seared Scallops 130

Beef Stir-Fry 131

Grilled Honey Lime Chicken 133

Baked Cod with Roasted Vegetables 135

Turkey Meatballs 136

Coconut Curry Shrimp 138

Lemon Herb Roasted Chicken 140

CHAPTER 6 SNACKS **142**

Caprese Skewers 143

Mini Quesadillas 144

Greek Yogurt Parfait 145

Bruschetta...146

Mini Stuffed Peppers 147

Smashed Avocado Toast 149

Mini Pita Pizzas 150

Veggie Spring Rolls 151

Spinach and Artichoke Dip 153

Fruit Kabobs...155

Stuffed Mushrooms 156

Salsa and Guacamole Duo 158

Chocolate-Dipped Strawberries 160

CHAPTER 7 DESSERTS RECIPES 161

Mini Berry Tarts 162

Chocolate Mug Cake 163

Individual Fruit Crumbles 165

Vegan Banana Split...167

Mini Apple Pies 168

Chocolate-Dipped Coconut Macaroons 170

Individual Chocolate Pudding Cups 172

Berry Parfait 174

Mini Cheesecakes 175

Grilled Pineapple with Coconut Whipped Cream..................................177

Chocolate-Dipped Strawberries 179

Chia Seed Pudding...180

CONCLUSION 181

INTRODUCTION

As we embark on a culinary journey through the Mediterranean, it's essential to understand the profound benefits that this diet offers for couples. Beyond its delicious flavors and aromatic spices, the Mediterranean diet has long been celebrated for its positive impact on physical health, mental well-being, and the overall vitality of individuals. When shared by couples, these benefits extend to strengthening the bond of love and togetherness, creating a foundation for a healthy and harmonious relationship.

1. **Heart-Healthy Nutrition:** The Mediterranean diet is renowned for its heart-healthy components, including an abundance of fruits, vegetables, whole grains, and olive oil. These ingredients, rich in antioxidants and essential nutrients, promote cardiovascular health, reducing the risk of heart disease for both partners and fostering a shared commitment to well-being.
2. **Aphrodisiacal Properties:** Certain elements of the Mediterranean diet, such as fresh seafood, nuts, and dark chocolate, are believed to possess aphrodisiacal qualities.

These natural aphrodisiacs can enhance romantic experiences and kindle the flames of passion, creating an intimate and sensual dining experience for couples.

3. **Mental Clarity and Emotional Well-Being:** The consumption of omega-3 fatty acids found in fish, as well as the abundance of fresh produce and healthy fats in the Mediterranean diet, is associated with improved cognitive function and emotional well-being. Couples who embrace this diet together may experience heightened mental clarity, emotional resilience, and a deeper sense of connection.

4. **Shared Culinary Experience:** The act of preparing and enjoying Mediterranean dishes together fosters a sense of collaboration, communication, and unity. From selecting fresh ingredients at the market to savoring a thoughtfully crafted meal, the process of cooking and dining as a couple can strengthen emotional bonds and create lasting memories.

5. **Longevity and Vitality:** Studies have shown that the Mediterranean diet is linked to increased longevity and overall vitality. By embracing this way of eating together, couples can aspire to lead longer, healthier lives, allowing them to cherish each other's company and continue creating cherished moments for years to come.

6. **Physical Well-Being and Energy:** The nutrient-dense nature of Mediterranean cuisine provides sustained energy and vitality, supporting an active and fulfilling lifestyle for couples. By sharing meals that prioritize fresh, wholesome ingredients, partners can cultivate a sense of physical well-being and energy, enabling them to partake in shared activities and adventures.

In essence, the benefits of the Mediterranean diet for couples extend beyond the realm of physical health, enriching the emotional, romantic, and spiritual aspects of their relationship. As partners embark on this gastronomic voyage together, they not only nourish their bodies but also nourish their love, creating a harmonious and enduring connection through the shared enjoyment of Mediterranean cuisine.

Chapter : Cooking Mediterranean Food Together at Home: Tips and Tricks

Embarking on a culinary adventure through Mediterranean cuisine can be an enriching and delightful experience for couples. Here are some tips and tricks to master the art of cooking Mediterranean food together at home:

1. **Embrace Olive Oil:** In Mediterranean cooking, olive oil is a staple ingredient. Swap out butter or other oils with extra-virgin olive oil for a healthier and authentic touch to your dishes. Whether it's for cooking, drizzling over pasta, or creating homemade salad dressings, the versatility of olive oil adds a distinctive Mediterranean flavor to your meals.

2. **Explore Fresh Ingredients:** Prioritize fresh, seasonal produce, herbs, and spices. Incorporate a variety of vegetables, such as tomatoes, cucumbers, onions, and bell peppers, to infuse vibrant colors and flavors into your dishes. Experiment with Mediterranean staples like chickpeas, lentils, and whole grains to add depth and nutrition to your meals.

3. **Savor Seafood:** Integrate seafood into your Mediterranean repertoire. Opt for nutrient-rich options like salmon, cod, or shrimp to add a touch of elegance and healthful benefits to your shared meals.

4. **Master the Art of Hummus:** Delight in the process of creating homemade creamy hummus with chickpeas and tahini. This beloved Mediterranean dip is a perfect addition to your culinary repertoire and can be a fun and collaborative cooking project for couples.

5. **Roast and Grill with Flair:** Experiment with roasting and grilling techniques to bring out the natural flavors of Mediterranean vegetables and proteins. Roasted cauliflower with lemon and cumin or sautéed shrimp and zucchini are just a few examples of dishes that can be prepared with a Mediterranean twist.

6. **Create Homemade Vinaigrettes:** Ditch store-bought dressings and craft your own vinaigrettes using olive oil, citrus, and herbs. This simple yet flavorful addition to your salads can elevate your dining experience and provide a sense of accomplishment when made together.

7. **Enjoy Wine in Moderation:** Embrace the Mediterranean tradition of enjoying wine in moderation as part of your culinary experience. Selecting the right wine to complement your Mediterranean dishes can add an extra layer of sophistication and enjoyment to your shared meals.

8. **Cooking as a Shared Experience:** Embrace the process of cooking together as a couple. Engage in meal preparation, from selecting fresh ingredients to collaborating on the cooking process. This shared experience fosters communication, teamwork, and the creation of cherished memories.

9. **Adapt Dishes When Eating Out:** When dining out, choose restaurants that offer Mediterranean-inspired dishes. Opt for grilled foods, fish or seafood as the main dish, and inquire if meals can be prepared using extra virgin olive oil. Adding vegetables and whole grain options to your order can further enhance your dining experience.

CHAPTER 1: BREAKFAST

CLASSIC OMELETTE

Prep Time: 5 minutes
Cooking Time: 10 minutes
Total Time: 15 minutes
Servings: 2

Ingredients:

- 4 large eggs
- 2 tablespoons milk
- Salt and pepper, to taste
- 2 tablespoons butter
- 1/4 cup of shredded cheddar or Swiss cheese
- Optional fillings: diced ham, sautéed mushrooms, onions, bell peppers, spinach, or any other desired ingredients

Directions:

1. Indulge in a symphony of flavors as you unite eggs, milk, salt, and pepper in a medium bowl. This exquisite fusion will captivate your palate with its enchanting medley.
2. To initiate the cooking process, place a non-stick skillet on medium heat and add a substantial amount of butter. Allow the butter to gradually melt, ensuring that it uniformly covers the entire surface of the skillet.
3. Gently pour the prepared egg mixture into the skillet, slightly angling it to ensure an even distribution of the mixture across the surface.
4. Once the edges of the omelette start to solidify, delicately raise them using a spatula and tilt the skillet slightly to enable the uncooked eggs to flow towards the outer edges.
5. When the omelette has achieved a mostly solid consistency, with a slightly runny surface, you can proceed to evenly distribute the shredded cheese and desired fillings onto a single side of the omelette.
6. Using a spatula, carefully fold the opposite side of the omelette over the filling, resulting in a delightful half-moon shape.
7. Allow the cooking process to continue for an additional 1-2 minutes, ensuring that the cheese has completely melted and the omelette has achieved the desired level of doneness according to your preference.
8. With a gentle touch, transfer the cooked omelette onto a plate and proceed to delicately divide it into two equal halves before serving.

Nutritional breakdown per serving:

Calories: 239 kcal, Protein: 14 grams, Carbohydrates: 2 grams, Fat: 19 grams, Saturated Fat: 6 grams, Cholesterol: 250 milligrams, Sodium: 297 milligrams, Fiber: 0 grams, and Sugar: 2 grams.

AVOCADO TOAST WITH POACHED EGGS

Prep Time: 10 minutes

Cooking Time: 10 minutes

Total Time: 20 minutes

Servings: 2

Ingredients:

- 2 large eggs
- 2 slices of whole-grain bread
- 1 ripe avocado
- 1 tablespoon lemon juice
- Salt and pepper, to taste
- Red pepper flakes (optional, for garnish)
- For an optional garnish, consider adding freshly chopped cilantro or parsley to enhance the presentation of the dish.

Directions:

1. To get started, grab a saucepan of medium size and fill it with water. Then, set the saucepan over medium heat and let the water come to a gentle simmer.
2. Begin by cracking an egg into a small bowl or ramekin. Carefully slide the egg into the gently simmering water and repeat the process with the second egg. Let the eggs cook without disturbance for approximately 3-4 minutes to achieve a soft, runny yolk, or extend the cooking time for a firmer yolk.
3. While the eggs poach, take the opportunity to toast the bread slices according to your preferred level of crispness.
4. Afterward, grab a small bowl and mix together the ripe avocado, lemon juice, salt, and pepper. Use a utensil to mash the ingredients until they are thoroughly combined and have a creamy texture.
5. Spread the mashed avocado evenly onto each slice of toasted bread.
6. When the eggs have cooked to your preferred level, carefully remove them from the water using a slotted spoon. Make sure to allow any excess water to drain off as you lift them out. Take caution to avoid any mishaps during this process.
7. Place one poached egg on top of each slice of avocado toast.
8. If you would like, feel free to enhance the flavor by adding additional salt, pepper, and red pepper flakes, adjusting the seasoning to align with your personal taste preferences.
9. For an appealing presentation, garnish the dish with chopped cilantro or parsley. This adds freshness and color. Serve immediately to enjoy the full flavors.

Nutritional breakdown per serving:

Calories: 312 kcal, Protein: 13 grams, Carbohydrates: 25 grams, Fat: 19 grams, Saturated Fat: 6 grams, Cholesterol: 150 milligrams, Sodium: 291 milligrams, Fiber: 10 grams, and Sugar: 3 grams.

PANCAKES

Prep Time: 10 minutes
Cooking Time: 10 minutes
Total Time: 20 minutes
Servings: 4 (2 pancakes per serving)

Ingredients:

- 1 1/2 cups all-purpose flour
- 3 1/2 teaspoons baking powder
- 1 tablespoon sugar
- 1/2 teaspoon salt
- 1 1/4 cups milk
- 1 large egg
- 3 tablespoons unsalted butter, melted
- Grease the pan with cooking spray or extra butter

Directions:

1. In a large mixing bowl, combine the flour, baking powder, sugar, and salt. Mix them well until they form a homogeneous mixture. Whisk the ingredients together until they are fully incorporated.
2. In order to achieve a uniform blend, begin by gathering the milk, egg, and melted butter in a distinct bowl. Utilize a whisk to effectively amalgamate the components until they are fully merged and evenly integrated.
3. To achieve a proper blending of the wet and dry ingredients, carefully pour them together and stir until they are just combined. It is crucial to avoid excessive mixing, as it is acceptable to have a few lumps remaining in the mixture.
4. Prior to cooking, ensure that the non-stick skillet or griddle is preheated to medium heat. Then, lightly apply a coating of either cooking spray or butter to the surface.
5. Pour about 1/4 cup of batter onto the skillet for each pancake, making sure to create a delicious result. Cook the pancake until bubbles form on the surface, indicating it's time to flip. Flip the pancake with caution and continue cooking for an extra 1-2 minutes until it achieves a beautiful golden brown color.
6. Proceed with the remaining batter, ensuring to add more cooking spray or butter as required.
7. Elevate the taste of the warm pancakes by adorning them with your preferred toppings, such as maple syrup, fresh berries, or whipped cream.

Nutritional breakdown per serving:

Calories: 285 kcal, Protein: 8 grams, Carbohydrates: 40 grams, Fat: 10 grams, Saturated Fat: 2 grams, Cholesterol: 100 milligrams, Sodium: 560 milligrams, Fiber: 1 grams, and Sugar: 20 grams.

OVERNIGHT CHIA PUDDING

Prep Time: 5 minutes

Chilling Time: Overnight (at least 6 hours)

Total Time: 6 hours 5 minutes

Servings: 2

Ingredients:

- 1 1/2 cups dairy-free milk (e.g., almond milk, coconut milk)
- 1/2 cup chia seeds
- 1-2 tablespoons maple syrup (adjust to taste)
- 1 teaspoon vanilla extract
- Optional toppings: fresh berries, sliced fruits, nuts, shredded coconut, honey, or granola

Directions:

1. Combine the dairy-free milk, chia seeds, maple syrup, and vanilla extract in a mixing bowl. Continuously whisk the mixture until the chia seeds are uniformly dispersed throughout.
2. To obtain a creamy pudding consistency, cover the bowl and refrigerate it for at least 6 hours or overnight. This will give the chia seeds enough time to fully absorb the liquid.
3. Once the chia pudding has been chilled, ensure a smooth texture by giving it a thorough stir to eliminate any clumps.
4. Divide the chia pudding into serving bowls or jars.
5. Customize your chia pudding by incorporating your favorite toppings, including fresh berries, sliced fruits, nuts, shredded coconut, honey, or granola.
6. Serve chilled and enjoy!

Nutritional breakdown per serving:

Calories: 235 kcal, Protein: 7 grams, Carbohydrates: 29 grams, Fat: 11 grams, Saturated Fat: 5 grams, Cholesterol: 5 milligrams, Sodium: 84 milligrams, Fiber: 16 grams, and Sugar: 8 grams.

BREAKFAST BURRITO

Prep Time: 15 minutes
Cooking Time: 15 minutes
Total Time: 30 minutes
Servings: 4

Ingredients:

- 8 large eggs
- 1/4 cup milk
- Salt and pepper, to taste
- 1 tablespoon butter or cooking oil
- 4 large flour tortillas
- 1 cup shredded cheddar cheese
- 4 slices cooked bacon, crumbled
- 1/2 cup diced bell peppers
- 1/2 cup diced onions
- Optional toppings: salsa, sour cream, avocado, cilantro

Directions:

1. To create a smooth mixture, start by placing eggs, milk, salt, and pepper into a mixing bowl. Use a whisk to vigorously combine the ingredients until they are thoroughly blended together.
2. Place a skillet on the stove and heat it over medium heat. Choose between butter or cooking oil and add it to the skillet. Add diced bell peppers and onions, sauté until soft and caramelized.
3. Carefully transfer the beaten eggs into the skillet containing the sautéed vegetables. Cook the mixture, stirring occasionally, until the eggs are scrambled and cooked to your liking. Take the skillet off the heat.
4. Warm the flour tortillas in a separate skillet or in the microwave for a few seconds to make them pliable.
5. Evenly distribute the scrambled eggs among the tortillas, placing them in the center of each one.
6. Add a generous portion of shredded cheddar cheese and crumbled bacon to the eggs, resulting in a delightful combination of flavors and textures. This effortless addition will take the dish to a whole new level of deliciousness.
7. Carefully fold the edges of the tortilla over the filling, and then tightly roll it up to create a burrito shape.

8. Optional: If desired, lightly toast the assembled burritos on a skillet or griddle for a few minutes to give them a crispy exterior.
9. Enjoy the warm breakfast burritos with your preferred toppings, such as salsa, sour cream, avocado, or cilantro.

Nutritional breakdown per serving:

Calories: 459 kcal, Protein: 23 grams, Carbohydrates: 26 grams, Fat: 29 grams, Saturated Fat: 8 grams, Cholesterol: 57 milligrams, Sodium: 717 milligrams, Fiber: 2 grams, and Sugar: 2 grams.

YOGURT PARFAIT

Prep Time: 10 minutes
Chilling Time: 1 hour (optional)
Total Time: 10 minutes (plus chilling time if desired)
Servings: 2

Ingredients:

- 2 cups Greek yogurt (plain or flavored)
- 1 cup fresh berries
- 1/2 cup granola
- Optional toppings: honey, shredded coconut, chopped nuts, or mint leaves

Directions:

1. When preparing your serving glasses or bowls, begin by evenly distributing half of the Greek yogurt into each container, placing it at the bottom as the first layer.
2. Place a generous amount of fresh berries on the surface of the yogurt.
3. Sprinkle a layer of granola over the berries.
4. Repeat the layers of yogurt, berries, and granola.
5. Optional: Drizzle honey over the top layer for added sweetness.
6. If you prefer, you can choose to cover the parfaits and refrigerate them for at least 1 hour. This will enable the flavors to mingle and the granola to achieve a slightly softer texture.
7. Before serving, garnish with shredded coconut, chopped nuts, or mint leaves, if desired.
8. Enjoy the yogurt parfaits immediately.

Nutritional breakdown per serving:

Calories: 300 kcal, Protein: 20 grams, Carbohydrates: 40 grams, Fat: 8 grams, Saturated Fat: 1 grams, Cholesterol: 0 milligrams, Sodium: 100 milligrams, Fiber: 5 grams, and Sugar: 20 grams.

FRENCH TOAST

Prep Time: 10 minutes
Cooking Time: 10 minutes
Total Time: 20 minutes
Servings: 4

Ingredients:

- 4 large eggs
- 1/2 cup milk
- 1 teaspoon vanilla extract
- 1/2 teaspoon ground cinnamon
- 8 slices of bread (such as brioche, challah, or French bread)
- Apply butter or cooking oil to the pan to prevent sticking
- Optional toppings include maple syrup, powdered sugar, fresh berries, and whipped cream.

Directions:

1. Combine the eggs, milk, vanilla extract, and ground cinnamon in a shallow dish, whisking them together until they are thoroughly mixed.
2. Prepare a large non-stick skillet or griddle by heating it over medium heat and greasing it with butter or cooking oil.
3. Gently place each slice of bread into the egg mixture, taking care to coat both sides evenly and allowing them to soak briefly.
4. Place the soaked bread slices onto the preheated skillet or griddle. Cook for 2-3 minutes on each side, or until golden brown and crispy.
5. Continue the process with the remaining bread slices, adjusting the amount of butter or oil in the pan as necessary.
6. Present the French toast while warm, accompanied by a selection of toppings of your preference, such as maple syrup, powdered sugar, fresh berries, or whipped cream.

Nutritional breakdown per serving:

Calories: 230 kcal, Protein: 11 grams, Carbohydrates: 26 grams, Fat: 9 grams, Saturated Fat: 1 grams, Cholesterol: 50 milligrams, Sodium: 280 milligrams, Fiber: 2 grams, and Sugar: 4 grams.

BREAKFAST QUESADILLAS

Prep Time: 10 minutes
Cooking Time: 10 minutes
Total Time: 20 minutes
Servings: 4

Ingredients:

- 8 large flour tortillas
- 8 large eggs
- 1/4 cup milk
- Salt and pepper, to taste
- 1 cup shredded cheddar cheese
- 1 cup diced cooked ham or bacon
- 1/2 cup diced bell peppers
- 1/2 cup diced onions
- Apply butter or cooking oil to the pan for greasing
- Optional toppings: salsa, sour cream, avocado, or cilantro

Directions:

1. In the skillet, mix the egg mixture with the sautéed vegetables. Cook the mixture, stirring occasionally, until the eggs are scrambled and cooked to your liking. Finally, remove the skillet from the heat source.
2. Begin by heating a large non-stick skillet or griddle over medium heat. Then, prepare the skillet or griddle for cooking by greasing it with either butter or cooking oil.
3. Take one tortilla and position it on the skillet. Proceed by evenly spreading a layer of shredded cheddar cheese atop the tortilla.
4. In a separate skillet, sauté the diced ham or bacon, bell peppers, and onions until the vegetables are softened.
5. Add a portion of the sautéed mixture on top of the cheese layer.
6. Pour a portion of the egg mixture over the sautéed mixture.
7. Place another tortilla on top to form a quesadilla.
8. Allow the tortilla to cook for approximately 2-3 minutes on each side, or until it reaches a desirable golden brown color and the cheese has completely melted.
9. Continue the process by repeating the same steps with the remaining tortillas and ingredients.
10. Cut each quesadilla into quarters or halves.
11. Serve the warm breakfast quesadillas with a variety of optional toppings, including salsa, sour cream, avocado, or cilantro, according to your preference.

Nutritional breakdown per serving:

Calories: 425 kcal, Protein: 24 grams, Carbohydrates: 34 grams, Fat: 22 grams, Saturated Fat: 20 grams, Cholesterol: 0 milligrams, Sodium: 780 milligrams, Fiber: 2 grams, and Sugar: 2 grams.

VEGGIE FRITTATA

Prep Time: 15 minutes
Cooking Time: 25 minutes
Total Time: 40 minutes
Servings: 6

Ingredients:

- 8 large eggs
- 1/4 cup milk
- Salt and pepper, to taste
- 1 tablespoon olive oil
- 1 cup diced bell peppers
- 1 cup diced onions
- 1 cup sliced mushrooms
- 1 cup chopped spinach
- 1 cup shredded cheddar cheese
- Optional toppings: fresh herbs, salsa, or hot sauce

Directions:

1. Before you begin, it is important to ensure that the oven has been preheated to a temperature of 375°F (190°C). This step is crucial to ensure optimal cooking results.
2. In a bowl, whisk together the eggs, milk, salt, and pepper until well combined. Set aside.
3. To start, heat a skillet that is oven-safe over medium heat and add olive oil. Allow the oil to warm up before proceeding further.
4. Next, add the diced bell peppers and onions to the skillet and cook them over medium heat until they become soft and tender, resulting in a delightful texture and flavor.
5. Once the sliced mushrooms and chopped spinach have been added to the skillet, proceed to cook them until the vegetables have reached a tender consistency and all excess moisture has evaporated.
6. Pour the egg mixture over the sautéed vegetables in the skillet. Stir gently to distribute the vegetables evenly.
7. Next, evenly distribute a generous amount of shredded cheddar cheese over the surface of the frittata.
8. Carefully move the skillet to the oven that has been preheated, and allow the frittata to bake for approximately 20-25 minutes. Keep an eye on it and remove it from the

oven once the eggs have set and the cheese has melted and developed a slight golden color.

9. Once you have taken the skillet out of the oven, it is important to let the frittata cool for a few minutes before serving.
10. To finish, divide the frittata into triangular portions and serve it while it is still warm.
11. Optional: Garnish with fresh herbs, salsa, or hot sauce.

Nutritional breakdown per serving:

Calories: 210 kcal, Protein: 14 grams, Carbohydrates: 7 grams, Fat: 14 grams, Saturated Fat: 3 grams, Cholesterol: 213 milligrams, Sodium: 280 milligrams, Fiber: 2 grams, and Sugar: 3 grams.

SMOOTHIE BOWL

Prep Time: 15 minutes
Cooking Time: 25 minutes
Total Time: 40 minutes
Servings: 6

Ingredients:

- 8 large eggs
- 1/4 cup milk
- Salt and pepper, to taste
- 1 tablespoon olive oil
- 1 cup diced bell peppers
- 1 cup diced onions
- 1 cup sliced mushrooms
- 1 cup chopped spinach
- 1 cup shredded cheddar cheese
- Optional toppings: fresh herbs, salsa, or hot sauce

Directions:

1. Before embarking on your culinary journey, it is imperative to verify that the oven has been preheated to a temperature of 375°F (190°C). This fundamental step lays the groundwork for achieving the best possible cooking outcomes.
2. In a bowl, whisk together the eggs, milk, salt, and pepper until well combined. Set aside.
3. To start, apply medium heat to an oven-safe skillet and heat up some olive oil. Ensure that the skillet is suitable for oven use before proceeding.
4. Incorporate the diced bell peppers and onions into the skillet and sauté them until they become tender, enhancing their flavors and textures.
5. Incorporate the sliced mushrooms and chopped spinach into the skillet. Cook the vegetables until they reach a tender consistency and any excess moisture has dissipated.
6. Pour the egg mixture over the sautéed vegetables in the skillet. Stir gently to distribute the vegetables evenly.
7. Generously scatter shredded cheddar cheese on the surface of the frittata.
8. Carefully transfer the skillet to the oven that has been preheated. Let it bake for approximately 20-25 minutes, ensuring that you monitor it closely. The eggs should be fully set, and the cheese should be melted and possess a pleasing golden color.

9. Gently remove the skillet from the oven and grant the frittata a short interval to cool down.
10. Cut the frittata into triangular wedges and serve it while still warm.
11. Optional: Garnish with fresh herbs, salsa, or hot sauce.

Nutritional breakdown per serving:

Calories: 210 kcal, Protein: 14 grams, Carbohydrates: 7 grams, Fat: 14 grams, Saturated Fat: 6 grams, Cholesterol: 2 milligrams, Sodium: 280 milligrams, Fiber: 2 grams, and Sugar: 3 grams.

BREAKFAST TACOS

Prep Time: 15 minutes
Cooking Time: 10 minutes
Total Time: 25 minutes
Servings: 4

Ingredients:

- 8 small flour tortillas
- 6 large eggs
- 1/4 cup milk
- Salt and pepper, to taste
- 1 tablespoon butter or cooking oil
- 1 cup diced bell peppers
- 1 cup diced onions
- 1 cup diced tomatoes
- 1 cup shredded cheddar cheese
- Optional toppings: salsa, avocado, cilantro, sour cream

Directions:

1. In a bowl, whisk together the eggs, milk, salt, and pepper until well combined. Set aside.
2. Warm up a generous amount of butter or cooking oil in a sizable skillet set to medium heat.
3. Introduce the diced bell peppers and onions into the skillet, then proceed to sauté them until they have achieved a softened texture.
4. Incorporate the diced tomatoes into the skillet and cook them for an extra 2 minutes, ensuring their flavors blend effortlessly with the other ingredients, creating a delightful symphony of tastes.
5. Gently transfer the egg mixture into the skillet, making sure it is spread out evenly. Proceed to combine and cook the eggs with the vegetables, ensuring they are thoroughly cooked until they reach the desired level of doneness.
6. Warm the flour tortillas either in a separate skillet or by using the microwave until they are thoroughly heated.
7. Place a portion of the scrambled eggs and vegetable mixture onto each tortilla.
8. To create a delicious layer of cheesy goodness, generously sprinkle shredded cheddar cheese over the cooked eggs, allowing it to melt and blend with the eggs.
9. Fold the tortillas in half or roll them up to form tacos.

10. Optional: Serve the breakfast tacos with salsa, avocado slices, cilantro, and sour cream on the side.

Nutritional breakdown per serving:

Calories: 320 kcal, Protein: 15 grams, Carbohydrates: 30 grams, Fat: 16 grams, Saturated Fat: 7 grams, Cholesterol: 50 milligrams, Sodium: 480 milligrams, Fiber: 3 grams, and Sugar: 4 grams.

BREAKFAST SANDWICH

Prep Time: 10 minutes
Cooking Time: 10 minutes
Total Time: 20 minutes
Servings: 2

Ingredients:

- 4 slices of bread (whole wheat, white, or your choice)
- 4 large eggs
- 4 slices of cooked bacon or ham
- 2 slices of cheese (cheddar, Swiss, or your choice)
- Apply butter or cooking oil to the pan to prevent sticking
- Optional toppings: sliced tomatoes, avocado, lettuce, mayonnaise, or mustard

Directions:

1. To begin, heat a large non-stick skillet or griddle over medium heat. Then, apply a coating of butter or cooking oil to grease the surface.
2. Begin by cracking the eggs into a bowl. Then, proceed to whisk the eggs vigorously until they are thoroughly beaten.
3. Preheat skillet or griddle. Pour beaten eggs onto surface. Cook until set, about 2-3 minutes. Flip and cook for 1-2 minutes.
4. While the eggs are cooking, take the opportunity to toast the bread slices.
5. After cooking the eggs, divide them into two portions and fold each portion in half to match the size of the bread slices.
6. Place a slice of cheese on top of each folded egg portion.
7. Construct the sandwiches by laying a slice of cooked bacon or ham onto one piece of bread. Top with the folded egg and cheese. Add any optional toppings, such as sliced tomatoes, avocado, lettuce, mayonnaise, or mustard. Finish with the second slice of bread.
8. Optional: Heat the assembled sandwiches in a panini press or in the skillet for a few minutes to melt the cheese and warm the sandwich.
9. Serve the breakfast sandwiches warm and enjoy!

Nutritional breakdown per serving:

Calories: 400 kcal, Protein: 25 grams, Carbohydrates: 26 grams, Fat: 22 grams, Saturated Fat: 9 grams, Cholesterol: 200 milligrams, Sodium: 800 milligrams, Fiber: 2 grams, and Sugar: 2 grams.

BANANA PANCAKES

Prep Time: 5 minutes

Cooking Time: 2-3 minutes per batch

Total Time: 10-15 minutes

Servings: 4 (8 small pancakes)

Ingredients:

- 1 ripe banana
- 2 large eggs, lightly beaten
- Cooking oil or butter (optional)
- Serve with maple syrup, jam, powdered sugar, or any other desired toppings
- Optional mix-ins (choose a few!):
- 1/8 teaspoon baking powder, for fluffier pancakes
- 1/8 tsp salt
- 1/4 tsp vanilla extract
- 1 tbsp unsweetened cocoa powder
- 1 tbsp honey
- 1/2 cup of chopped nuts, chocolate chips, or a combination
- 1/2 cup granola
- 1 cup of fresh fruit options include blueberries, raspberries, or chopped apples

Directions:

1. Using a small bowl, mash the ripe banana until it reaches a smooth consistency.
2. Ensure a thorough mixture by combining the mashed banana and lightly beaten eggs together.
3. Optional: Add any desired mix-ins, such as baking powder, salt, vanilla extract, cocoa powder, honey, nuts, chocolate chips, granola, or fresh fruit. Mix until well combined.
4. To prepare for cooking, preheat a non-stick skillet or griddle over medium heat. If desired, you can choose to grease the skillet with butter or oil.
5. For each pancake, pour about 1/4 cup of batter onto the skillet while cooking.
6. Place the pancakes on the heat source and cook them for around 2-3 minutes. Keep an eye out for the formation of bubbles on the surface as an indication of readiness.
7. After cooking one side of the pancakes, carefully flip them over and cook for an additional 2-3 minutes until they achieve a desired golden brown color and are thoroughly cooked inside.

8. Continue the process with the remaining batter, making sure to add additional butter or oil to the skillet as necessary.
9. Serve the banana pancakes warm with your choice of toppings, such as maple syrup, jam, powdered sugar, or any other desired toppings.

Nutritional breakdown per serving (2 small pancakes):

Calories: 150 kcal, Protein: 7 grams, Carbohydrates: 18 grams, Fat: 6 grams, Saturated Fat: 2 grams, Cholesterol: 55 milligrams, Sodium: 100 milligrams, Fiber: 2 grams, and Sugar: 9 grams.

BREAKFAST QUINOA BOWL

Prep Time: 5 minutes

Cooking Time: 15 minutes

Total Time: 20 minutes

Servings: 2

Ingredients:

- 1 cup cooked quinoa
- 1 ripe banana, sliced
- 1/4 cup chopped nuts
- 2 tablespoons honey or maple syrup
- 1/2 teaspoon cinnamon
- Apply cooking spray or butter to grease the muffin tin

Directions:

1. In a small saucepan, heat the cooked quinoa over medium heat until warmed through.
2. Divide the warm quinoa into two bowls.
3. Top each bowl of quinoa with sliced bananas and chopped nuts.
4. To elevate the taste of the quinoa, you can enhance its flavor by gently drizzling it with either honey or maple syrup.
5. Sprinkle cinnamon over the top.
6. Optional: Add any additional toppings you desire, such as fresh berries, sliced fruits, yogurt, chia seeds, or coconut flakes.
7. Serve the breakfast quinoa bowls warm and enjoy!

Nutritional breakdown per serving:

Calories: 300 kcal, Protein: 7 grams, Carbohydrates: 55 grams, Fat: 8 grams, Saturated Fat: 1 grams, Cholesterol: 5 milligrams, Sodium: 5 milligrams, Fiber: 6 grams, and Sugar: 23 grams.

EGG AND VEGGIE MUFFIN CUPS

Prep Time: 10 minutes
Cooking Time: 20 minutes
Total Time: 30 minutes
Servings: 6 muffin cups

Ingredients:

- 6 large eggs
- 1/4 cup milk
- Salt and pepper, to taste
- 1/2 cup diced bell peppers
- 1/2 cup diced onions
- 1/2 cup diced tomatoes
- 1/2 cup chopped spinach
- 1/2 cup shredded cheddar cheese
- Cooking spray or butter, for greasing the muffin tin

Directions:

1. To begin, ensure that you preheat the oven to 350°F (175°C). Once the oven is preheated, proceed to grease the muffin tin using either cooking spray or butter.
2. In a bowl, whisk together the eggs, milk, salt, and pepper until well combined.
3. Divide the diced bell peppers, onions, tomatoes, chopped spinach, and shredded cheddar cheese evenly among the muffin cups.
4. With caution, pour the egg mixture over the vegetables and cheese in each muffin cup, making sure to fill them up to approximately 3/4 of their capacity.
5. Gently stir the ingredients in each muffin cup to ensure they are evenly distributed.
6. Once you have placed the muffin tin in the preheated oven, let them bake for approximately 20 minutes. While they are baking, it is crucial to keep an eye on their progress. Once the muffin cups are fully set and display a gentle, golden color on top, carefully remove them from the oven.
7. Once you have taken the muffin tin out of the oven, it is important to give the muffin cups a few minutes to cool down before handling them. This precautionary measure will effectively prevent any potential burns or discomfort that may arise from touching or removing the muffins.
8. When removing the muffin cups from the tin, begin by gently loosening the edges of each cup using a butter knife. Once the edges are loosened, carefully lift and extract the muffin cups from the tin.
9. Serve the egg and veggie muffin cups warm and enjoy!

Nutritional breakdown per serving (1 muffin cup):

Calories: 110 kcal, Protein: 8 grams, Carbohydrates: 4 grams, Fat: 7 grams, Saturated Fat: 3 grams, Cholesterol: 100 milligrams, Sodium: 150 milligrams, Fiber: 1 grams, and Sugar: 2 grams.

CHAPTER 2: LUNCH RECIPES

CAPRESE SALAD

Prep Time: 10 minutes
Cooking Time: 20 minutes
Total Time: 30 minutes
Servings: 6 muffin cups

Ingredients:

- 6 large eggs
- 1/4 cup milk
- Salt and pepper, to taste
- 1/2 cup diced bell peppers
- 1/2 cup diced onions
- 1/2 cup diced tomatoes
- 1/2 cup chopped spinach
- 1/2 cup shredded cheddar cheese
- Grease the muffin tin using cooking spray or butter, both are suitable options

Directions:

1. To initiate the baking process, start by preheating your oven to 350°F (175°C). Following that, apply a generous layer of cooking spray or butter to the muffin tin to prevent the baked goods from sticking.
2. To ensure a thorough combination and blending of the mixture, whisk the eggs, milk, salt, and pepper together in a bowl.
3. Divide the diced bell peppers, onions, tomatoes, chopped spinach, and shredded cheddar cheese evenly among the muffin cups.
4. Ensure that each muffin cup is filled up to about 3/4 full by pouring the egg mixture over the vegetables and cheese.
5. Gently stir the ingredients in each muffin cup to ensure they are evenly distributed.
6. Bake the muffin cups in the preheated oven for about 20 minutes, or until they are completely cooked through and achieve a gentle golden hue on the top.
7. Once the muffin tin has been taken out of the oven, it is recommended to let the muffin cups cool for a short duration.
8. Gently loosen the edges of the muffin cups using a butter knife, and then proceed to remove them from the tin.
9. Serve the egg and veggie muffin cups warm and enjoy!

Nutritional breakdown per serving (1 muffin cup):

Calories: 110 kcal, Protein: 8 grams, Carbohydrates: 4 grams, Fat: 7 grams, Saturated Fat: 3 grams, Cholesterol: 30 milligrams, Sodium: 150 milligrams, Fiber: 1 grams, and Sugar: 2 grams.

CHICKPEA SALAD WRAPS

Prep Time: 15 minutes
Cooking Time: 0 minutes
Total Time: 15 minutes
Servings: 4 wraps

Ingredients:

- 2 cups cooked chickpeas, drained and rinsed
- 1/4 cup diced red onion
- 1/4 cup diced cucumber
- 1/4 cup diced bell peppers
- 1/4 cup diced tomatoes
- 1/4 cup chopped fresh parsley
- 2 tablespoons lemon juice
- 2 tablespoons extra-virgin olive oil
- 1 teaspoon ground cumin
- Salt and pepper, to taste
- 4 large whole wheat tortillas or wraps
- Optional toppings: avocado slices, lettuce, sprouts, or hummus

Directions:

1. In a large bowl, combine the chickpeas, red onion, cucumber, bell peppers, tomatoes, parsley, lemon juice, olive oil, cumin, salt, and pepper. Mix well to combine all the ingredients.
2. Lay out the tortillas or wraps on a clean surface.
3. Evenly distribute the chickpea salad mixture among the tortillas, ensuring that it is placed in the center of each individual tortilla.
4. Optional: Add any desired toppings, such as avocado slices, lettuce, sprouts, or hummus.
5. Begin by folding the sides of the tortillas over the filling, and then proceed to roll them up tightly, creating wraps.
6. If preferred, it is possible to slice each wrap in half diagonally before serving.

Nutritional breakdown per serving (1 wrap):

Calories: 300 kcal, Protein: 10 grams, Carbohydrates: 40 grams, Fat: 12 grams, Saturated Fat: 4 grams, Cholesterol: 2 milligrams, Sodium: 400 milligrams, Fiber: 8 grams, and Sugar: 4 grams.

QUINOA SALAD WITH ROASTED VEGETABLES

Prep Time: 15 minutes
Cooking Time: 40 minutes
Total Time: 55 minutes
Servings: 4

Ingredients:

- 1 cup quinoa, cooked and cooled
- 1 cup cherry tomatoes, halved
- 1 cup bell peppers, diced
- 1 cup zucchini, diced
- 1 cup red onion, sliced
- 2 tablespoons olive oil
- 1 teaspoon dried oregano
- 1/2 teaspoon garlic powder
- Salt and pepper, to taste
- 4 cups mixed greens
- 1/4 cup crumbled feta cheese (optional)
- Lemon wedges, for serving

For the Lemon Herb Vinaigrette:

- 3 tablespoons extra-virgin olive oil
- 2 tablespoons lemon juice
- 1 tablespoon fresh parsley, chopped
- 1 tablespoon fresh basil, chopped
- 1 teaspoon honey or maple syrup
- Salt and pepper, to taste

Directions:

1. To prepare for baking, preheat your oven to 400°F (200°C). Next, apply a coat of cooking spray or butter to the muffin tin to prevent sticking.
2. Combine the cherry tomatoes, bell peppers, zucchini, and red onion in a large bowl. To evenly coat the mixture, drizzle olive oil over it and sprinkle with dried oregano, garlic powder, salt, and pepper. Toss the vegetables to distribute the seasonings.
3. To achieve a delicious roast, place the vegetables on a baking sheet and cook them in a preheated oven for approximately 40 minutes. Stir every 15 minutes for even

browning and tenderness. Once browned and tender, cool for 10 minutes before serving.

4. For the lemon herb vinaigrette, combine the olive oil, lemon juice, parsley, basil, honey or maple syrup, salt, and pepper in a separate bowl. Whisk the ingredients together until well blended.

5. To prepare a delicious salad, start by placing the cooked quinoa, roasted vegetables, and mixed greens in a large salad bowl. Next, generously drizzle the lemon herb vinaigrette over the ingredients. Finally, gently toss everything together to ensure all the flavors are well combined.

6. Optional: Sprinkle crumbled feta cheese over the salad.

7. Serve the quinoa salad with roasted vegetables at room temperature or chilled, with lemon wedges on the side.

Nutritional breakdown per serving:

Calories: 5 kcal, Protein: 7 grams, Carbohydrates: 32 grams, Fat: 16 grams, Saturated Fat: 2 grams, Cholesterol: 30 milligrams, Sodium: 150 milligrams, Fiber: 6 grams, and Sugar: 6 grams.

MEDITERRANEAN HUMMUS BOWL

Prep Time: 15 minutes
Cooking Time: 0 minutes
Total Time: 15 minutes
Servings: 4

Ingredients:

- 1 cup cooked brown rice
- 1 cup cherry tomatoes, sliced
- 1/2 cup diced red onion
- 1/2 cup sliced cucumber
- 1/2 cup crumbled feta cheese
- 1 cup chickpeas, drained and rinsed
- 1 tablespoon garlic herb seasoning
- 1/4 cup hummus (classic or your preferred flavor)
- Optional toppings: lemon wedges, fresh parsley, olive oil, hot sauce

Directions:

1. To create a delightful combination, combine the cooked brown rice, cherry tomatoes, red onion, cucumber, feta cheese, and chickpeas in a spacious bowl. Mix them together until well blended.
2. Sprinkle the garlic herb seasoning over the mixture and toss to evenly coat the ingredients.
3. To create an appealing presentation, transfer the hummus onto a plate or bowl using a spoon. Then, use the back of the spoon to spread it out, forming beautiful swirls.
4. Arrange the rest of the ingredients on the hummus as per your preference.
5. Optional: Drizzle with olive oil, squeeze fresh lemon juice, and add a dash of hot sauce for extra flavor.
6. Serve the Mediterranean hummus bowls immediately and enjoy!

Nutritional breakdown per serving:

Calories: 350 kcal, Protein: 12 grams, Carbohydrates: 49 grams, Fat: 12 grams, Saturated Fat: 1 grams, Cholesterol: 0 milligrams, Sodium: 450 milligrams, Fiber: 8 grams, and Sugar: 4 grams.

AVOCADO TOAST

Prep Time: 5 minutes
Cooking Time: 0 minutes
Total Time: 5 minutes
Servings: 2

Ingredients:

- 1 ripe avocado
- 2 slices of whole-wheat bread
- 1 tablespoon fresh cilantro, chopped
- 1/2 lime, juiced
- Pinch of red pepper flakes (optional)
- Salt and pepper, to taste

Directions:

1. Put the slices of bread into a toaster and toast them until they reach a delightful golden brown color, becoming crispy in the process.
2. Begin by cutting the avocado in half. Next, carefully remove the pit, and using a spoon, scoop the creamy flesh into a bowl.
3. Using a fork, continue to mash the avocado until it reaches the desired consistency that you prefer.
4. Using a fork, mash the avocado to achieve the desired consistency. Then, incorporate the chopped cilantro, lime juice, red pepper flakes (if desired), salt, and pepper into the mashed avocado. Make sure to mix the ingredients thoroughly, ensuring that all the flavors are well incorporated.
5. Evenly distribute the avocado mixture onto each slice of toasted bread.
6. Optional: Garnish with additional cilantro or a sprinkle of red pepper flakes.
7. Serve the avocado toast immediately and enjoy!

Nutritional breakdown per serving:

Calories: 200 kcal, Protein: 5 grams, Carbohydrates: 18 grams, Fat: 13 grams, Saturated Fat: 2 grams, Cholesterol: 3 milligrams, Sodium: 200 milligrams, Fiber: 8 grams, and Sugar: 0 grams.

VEGGIE WRAP

Prep Time: 15 minutes
Cooking Time: 0 minutes
Total Time: 15 minutes
Servings: 2 wraps

Ingredients:

- 2 large whole wheat tortillas or wraps
- 1/2 cup hummus (classic or your preferred flavor)
- 1/2 cup shredded carrots
- 1/2 cup sliced bell peppers
- 1/2 cup sliced cucumbers
- 1/4 cup sliced red onion
- 1/4 cup sliced avocado
- Handful of fresh spinach or lettuce leaves
- Salt and pepper, to taste

Directions:

1. Lay out the tortillas or wraps on a clean surface.
2. Evenly distribute a liberal quantity of hummus on each tortilla, ensuring to leave a slight margin around the periphery.
3. Layer the shredded carrots, sliced bell peppers, cucumbers, red onion, avocado, and fresh spinach or lettuce leaves on top of the hummus.
4. Sprinkle with salt and pepper to taste.
5. After spreading a generous amount of hummus evenly onto each tortilla, leave a small border around the edges. Next, fold the sides of the tortillas over the filling, and tightly roll them up to create wraps.
6. Before serving, you can choose to cut each wrap diagonally in half if you prefer.

Nutritional breakdown per serving (1 wrap):

Calories: 250 kcal, Protein: 8 grams, Carbohydrates: 35 grams, Fat: 10 grams, Saturated Fat: 1 grams, Cholesterol: 0 milligrams, Sodium: 400 milligrams, Fiber: 9 grams, and Sugar: 4 grams.

SPINACH AND FETA STUFFED BELL PEPPERS

Prep Time: 15 minutes
Cooking Time: 35 minutes
Total Time: 50 minutes
Servings: 4

Ingredients:

- 4 large bell peppers (any color)
- 1 tablespoon olive oil
- 1 small onion, finely chopped
- 2 cloves garlic, minced
- 4 cups fresh spinach, chopped
- 1/2 cup crumbled feta cheese
- 1/4 cup grated Parmesan cheese
- Salt and pepper, to taste

Directions:

1. To prepare for baking, preheat your oven to 350°F (175°C). Next, apply a coat of cooking spray or butter to the muffin tin to prevent sticking.
2. After cutting off the tops of the bell peppers, take the time to remove the seeds and membranes. Once complete, set the prepared bell peppers aside for later use.
3. To initiate the cooking process, heat the olive oil in a generously-sized skillet over medium heat. Following that, introduce the chopped onion and minced garlic to the skillet and proceed to sauté the mixture until the onion achieves a translucent appearance and emits an enticing fragrance.
4. Next, incorporate the chopped spinach into the skillet and cook it until it wilts, which typically takes around 2 to 3 minutes. Once the desired wilting is achieved, remove the skillet from the heat source.
5. In a mixing bowl, combine the cooked spinach mixture, crumbled feta cheese, grated Parmesan cheese, salt, and pepper. Stir until well combined.
6. Stuff each bell pepper with the spinach and feta mixture, pressing it down gently to fill the peppers evenly.
7. In a baking dish, carefully place the stuffed bell peppers ensuring they are evenly arranged. Proceed to cover the bell peppers with foil, ensuring they are securely protected.
8. After placing the baking dish containing the stuffed bell peppers in the oven that has been preheated, allow them to bake for approximately 25 minutes.

9. Once this time has elapsed, carefully remove the foil covering and continue baking for an additional 10 minutes, or until the peppers attain a tender texture and the cheese becomes melted with a delightful, slightly golden shade.
10. Remove from the oven and let cool for a few minutes before serving.

Nutritional breakdown per serving:

Calories: 150 kcal, Protein: 7 grams, Carbohydrates: 15 grams, Fat: 8 grams, Saturated Fat: 3 grams, Cholesterol: 27 milligrams, Sodium: 300 milligrams, Fiber: 4 grams, and Sugar: 7 grams.

VEGAN BUDDHA BOWL

Prep Time: 20 minutes
Cooking Time: 20 minutes
Total Time: 40 minutes
Servings: 4-6

Ingredients:

- Buddha Bowl Components:
- Whole grains (e.g., brown rice, quinoa, farro)
- Vegan protein (e.g., tofu, tempeh, beans, or legumes)
- Fresh vegetables (e.g., cabbage, kale, spinach, cucumbers, carrots, bell peppers)
- Microgreens
- Seeds or nuts
- Dressing or sauce of your choice

Instructions:

1. Start by cooking your choice of whole grains according to the package instructions. To save time, this task can be completed ahead of time and the prepared dish can be stored in the refrigerator until needed.
2. While the grains are cooking, prepare the other components of the Buddha bowl.
3. Choose your vegan protein source and prepare it according to your preference (e.g., sautéed tofu, roasted chickpeas, marinated tempeh).
4. Wash and chop the fresh vegetables, including cabbage, kale, spinach, cucumbers, carrots, and bell peppers.
5. Prepare any additional toppings you desire, such as microgreens, seeds, or nuts.
6. Assemble the Buddha bowls by dividing the cooked whole grains among the bowls as the base.
7. Arrange the vegan protein, fresh vegetables, microgreens, and toppings on top of the grains.
8. Drizzle your preferred dressing or sauce over the Buddha bowls.
9. Serve the vegan Buddha bowls immediately and enjoy!

Nutritional breakdown per serving:

Calories: 450 kcal, Protein: 20 grams, Carbohydrates: 70 grams, Fat: 20 grams, Saturated Fat: 5 grams, Cholesterol: 0 milligrams, Sodium: 400 milligrams, Fiber: 15 grams, and Sugar: 6 grams.

MARGHERITA PANINI

Prep Time: 10 minutes
Cooking Time: 10 minutes
Total Time: 20 minutes
Servings: 2

Ingredients:

- 4 slices of crusty bread (such as ciabatta or sourdough)
- 4 tablespoons tomato sauce or marinara sauce
- 4 ounces fresh mozzarella cheese, sliced
- 1 large tomato, sliced
- Fresh basil leaves
- Olive oil, for brushing
- Salt and pepper, to taste

Directions:

1. Before starting the cooking process, ensure that the panini press or grill pan is preheated to a medium heat.
2. On a clean surface, carefully arrange the slices of bread in a single layer.
3. Take each slice of bread and evenly spread 1 tablespoon of tomato sauce over its surface.
4. Layer the mozzarella cheese, tomato slices, and fresh basil leaves on top of the sauce.
5. Season with salt and pepper to taste.
6. Place the remaining slices of bread on top to create sandwiches.
7. To ensure an even distribution, use a brush to coat the outer sides of the sandwiches with olive oil.
8. Carefully place the sandwiches in the preheated panini press or grill pan to begin the cooking process.
9. Allow the sandwiches to cook for approximately 4-5 minutes, or until the bread achieves a golden brown color and the cheese has melted to perfection.
10. Remove the panini from the press or pan and let them cool for a minute.
11. Slice the panini in half diagonally, if desired, and serve.

Nutritional breakdown per serving:

Calories: 350 kcal, Protein: 16 grams, Carbohydrates: 38 grams, Fat: 15 grams, Saturated Fat: 7 grams, Cholesterol: 50 milligrams, Sodium: 600 milligrams, Fiber: 4 grams, and Sugar: 5 grams.

LENTIL AND VEGETABLE STIR-FRY

Prep Time: 10 minutes
Cooking Time: 20 minutes
Total Time: 30 minutes
Servings: 4

Ingredients:

- 1 cup dried lentils
- 2 cups vegetable broth
- 1 tablespoon olive oil
- 1 onion, sliced
- 2 cloves garlic, minced
- 1 red bell pepper, sliced
- 1 zucchini, sliced
- 1 cup broccoli florets
- 1 cup snap peas
- 2 tablespoons soy sauce
- 1 tablespoon rice vinegar
- 1 teaspoon sesame oil
- 1/2 teaspoon ginger powder
- Salt and pepper, to taste
- Optional: Sesame seeds can be used for garnishing
- Optional: Fresh cilantro or green onions can be used for garnishing

Directions:

1. Rinse the lentils under cold water and drain.
2. Begin the lentil preparation by heating a medium saucepan and bringing the vegetable broth to a boil. Once boiling, add the lentils to the saucepan and reduce the heat to low. Allow the lentils to simmer for around 15-20 minutes until they reach a tender consistency. After cooking, carefully drain any excess liquid and set the cooked lentils aside for later use.
3. In a large skillet or wok, heat the olive oil over medium heat. Add the sliced onion and minced garlic. Sauté for 2-3 minutes until the onion becomes translucent.
4. Next, add the sliced bell pepper, zucchini, broccoli florets, and snap peas to the skillet. Stir-fry the vegetables for approximately 5-7 minutes, or until they reach a crisp-tender texture.

5. In a small bowl, whisk together the soy sauce, rice vinegar, sesame oil, ginger powder, salt, and pepper.
6. Create space in the skillet by pushing the vegetables to one side. On the other side, add the cooked lentils. Proceed by pouring the sauce over the lentils and vegetables. To achieve a harmonious blend and ensure the ingredients are evenly coated with the sauce, it is important to stir everything together thoroughly.
7. Cook for an additional 2-3 minutes, or until everything is heated through.
8. For added flavor and aesthetic appeal, you may choose to enhance the dish by adding a finishing touch. After removing it from the heat, consider garnishing with sesame seeds, fresh cilantro, or green onions, according to your preference.
9. Serve the lentil and vegetable stir-fry as is or over a bed of cooked rice or noodles.

Nutritional breakdown per serving:

Calories: 250 kcal, Protein: 14 grams, Carbohydrates: 40 grams, Fat: 5 grams, Saturated Fat: 1 grams, Cholesterol: 1 milligrams, Sodium: 600 milligrams, Fiber: 15 grams, and Sugar: 7 grams.

MEXICAN QUINOA STUFFED PEPPERS

Prep Time: 15 minutes
Cooking Time: 30 minutes
Total Time: 45 minutes
Servings: 4

Ingredients:

- 1 cup quinoa, rinsed and drained
- 2 cups vegetable broth
- 4 large bell peppers, any color
- 1 tablespoon olive oil
- 1 small onion, diced
- 2 cloves garlic, minced
- 1 jalapeño pepper, seeded and minced (optional for spice)
- 1 cup corn kernels (fresh or frozen)
- 15-ounce can of black beans, making sure to rinse and drain them beforehand
- 1 teaspoon chili powder
- 1/2 teaspoon cumin
- Salt and pepper, to taste
- 1 cup of shredded Mexican blend cheese in your recipe, or use a vegan cheese alternative if preferred
- Fresh cilantro, for garnish (optional)

Directions:

1. To prepare for baking, start by preheating your oven to 350°F (175°C). Then, ensure the muffin tin is well-prepared by applying a layer of cooking spray or butter to prevent any sticking.
2. Place the vegetable broth in a saucepan and heat it until it begins to boil. Next, add the quinoa to the saucepan and reduce the heat to a gentle simmer.
3. After covering the saucepan, let the quinoa cook for approximately 15 minutes, or until it has absorbed all the liquid and achieved a tender texture. Once cooked, set it aside for future use.
4. Start by removing the tops of the bell peppers and discarding the seeds and membranes. Next, place the peppers in a baking dish, ensuring that the cut side is facing up, and set them aside for future use.

5. In a large skillet, heat the olive oil over medium heat. Add the diced onion, minced garlic, and jalapeño pepper (if using). Sauté for 3-4 minutes until the onion becomes translucent.
6. Add the corn kernels, black beans, chili powder, cumin, salt, and pepper to the skillet. Mix the ingredients together thoroughly and continue cooking for an extra 2 to 3 minutes.
7. Remove the skillet from heat and stir in the cooked quinoa.
8. With the help of a spoon, generously stuff the bell peppers with the quinoa mixture, making sure to fill them all the way to the top. Use gentle pressure to press down on the filling, compacting it as you go.
9. Ensure an equal distribution of the shredded cheese as you sprinkle it over the stuffed peppers.
10. Once the baking dish is securely covered with aluminum foil, carefully transfer it into the oven that has been preheated. Allow the dish to bake for approximately 20 minutes, ensuring even cooking.
11. Remove the aluminum foil and proceed to bake for an additional 5-10 minutes, or until the cheese has completely melted and developed a bubbly texture.
12. Remove from the oven and let the stuffed peppers cool for a few minutes.
13. Optionally, you can enhance the presentation by adding a garnish of fresh cilantro before serving.

Nutritional breakdown per serving:

Calories: 350 kcal, Protein: 15 grams, Carbohydrates: 55 grams, Fat: 10 grams, Saturated Fat: 4 grams, Cholesterol: 0 milligrams, Sodium: 600 milligrams, Fiber: 12 grams, and Sugar: 7 grams.

GREEK SALAD PITA POCKETS

Prep Time: 15 minutes
Cooking Time: None (assembly only)
Total Time: 15 minutes
Servings: 4

Ingredients:

Salad:

- 1 cup chopped Romaine lettuce
- 1/2 cup chopped red onion
- 2 cups chopped bell peppers
- 1 cup chopped cucumbers
- 3 oz. Feta cheese, crumbled
- 2 tablespoons chopped fresh parsley

Dressing:

- 1 tablespoon olive oil
- 2 tablespoons lemon juice
- 1 teaspoon dried oregano
- Pepper, to taste

Pitas:

- 4 whole-grain pita rounds

Directions:

1. In a large bowl, combine the chopped Romaine lettuce, red onion, bell peppers, cucumbers, crumbled Feta cheese, and fresh parsley to make the salad.
2. In a small bowl, whisk together the olive oil, lemon juice, dried oregano, and pepper to make the dressing.
3. Carefully pour the dressing over the salad, ensuring that all the ingredients are evenly coated, and gently toss to combine.
4. Cut the whole-grain pita rounds in half to create pockets.
5. Fill each pita half with the dressed salad mixture.
6. Serve the Greek salad pita pockets immediately and enjoy!

Nutritional breakdown per serving:

Calories: 265 kcal, Protein: 7 grams, Carbohydrates: 38 grams, Fat: 9 grams, Saturated Fat: 3.5 grams, Cholesterol: 5 milligrams, Sodium: 430 milligrams, Fiber: 4 grams, and Sugar: 0 grams.

VEGAN CHICKPEA CURRY

Prep Time: 10 minutes
Cooking Time: 30 minutes
Total Time: 40 minutes
Servings: 4

Ingredients:

- 2 tablespoons vegetable oil or coconut oil
- 1 medium onion, sliced
- 3 cloves garlic, minced
- 1 teaspoon crushed red pepper flakes
- 1-2 tablespoons curry powder
- 1 teaspoon cumin
- 1 (15 ounce) can crushed tomatoes
- 1 (13.5 ounce) can coconut milk
- 2 (15 ounce) cans chickpeas, drained and rinsed
- Salt and pepper, to taste
- Optionally, garnish with chopped fresh cilantro and lime wedges
- Naan bread and rice, to serve (optional)

Directions:

1. Start by positioning a pot or skillet on the stovetop and adjusting the heat to medium. Proceed to introduce either vegetable oil or coconut oil into the pot or skillet, ensuring it is evenly distributed, and allow it to heat up thoroughly.
2. Next, incorporate the sliced onion and minced garlic into the pot. Sauté the mixture for approximately 3 to 4 minutes, or until the onion achieves a translucent appearance.
3. After that, carefully stir in the crushed red pepper flakes, curry powder, and cumin. Continue cooking the mixture for an extra minute, allowing the spices to toast and fully develop their flavors.
4. Add the crushed tomatoes and coconut milk to the pot. Stir well to combine.
5. Gradually increase the heat until the mixture achieves a gentle simmer, taking care to avoid boiling. Let it cook for about 10 minutes, ensuring to stir occasionally for uniform cooking.
6. Introduce the drained and rinsed chickpeas to the pot, ensuring they are evenly distributed. Stir the mixture well to coat the chickpeas thoroughly with the flavorsome curry sauce.

7. Season with salt and pepper to taste.
8. Continue to simmer the curry for another 10-15 minutes, allowing the flavors to meld together.
9. Take the pot off the heat and allow the curry to rest for a few minutes, allowing the flavors to meld together.
10. If desired, present the vegan chickpea curry while it's still hot, and add a flavorful touch by garnishing it with freshly chopped cilantro and lime wedges.
11. Accompany with naan bread and rice, if desired.

Nutritional breakdown per serving:

Calories: 380 kcal, Protein: 12 grams, Carbohydrates: 42 grams, Fat: 20 grams, Saturated Fat: 14 grams, Cholesterol: 2 milligrams, Sodium: 480 milligrams, Fiber: 10 grams, and Sugar: 8 grams.

CAPRESE PANZANELLA SALAD

Prep Time: 15 minutes
Cooking Time: None
Total Time: 15 minutes
Servings: 4

Ingredients:

- 4 cups day-old crusty bread, cut into cubes
- 2 cups cherry tomatoes, halved
- 8 oz. fresh mozzarella cheese, cubed
- 1/2 cup fresh basil leaves, torn
- 2 tablespoons extra-virgin olive oil
- 2 tablespoons balsamic vinegar
- Salt and pepper, to taste

Directions:

1. In a large bowl, combine the bread cubes, cherry tomatoes, fresh mozzarella cheese, and torn basil leaves.
2. Carefully pour the extra-virgin olive oil and balsamic vinegar onto the salad, ensuring that it is evenly coated.
3. Season with salt and pepper to taste.
4. Toss the ingredients gently until well combined, making sure the bread is coated with the dressing.
5. Allow the salad to rest for a brief period, giving the flavors an opportunity to blend harmoniously.
6. Serve the Caprese Panzanella Salad immediately and enjoy!

Nutritional breakdown per serving:

Calories: 320 kcal, Protein: 15 grams, Carbohydrates: 27 grams, Fat: 17 grams, Saturated Fat: 7 grams, Cholesterol: 6 milligrams, Sodium: 430 milligrams, Fiber: 2 grams, and Sugar: 4grams.

VEGGIE SUSHI ROLLS

Prep Time: 30 minutes
Cooking Time: None
Total Time: 30 minutes
Servings: Makes 4-6 rolls (depending on size)

Ingredients:

- 2 cups sushi rice
- 4-6 nori seaweed sheets
- Assorted vegetables (e.g., cucumber, avocado, bell peppers, carrots, radishes, etc.), julienned or thinly sliced
- Soy sauce, for dipping
- Pickled ginger and wasabi, for serving (optional)

Directions:

1. Prepare the sushi rice following the instructions provided on the package. Once the cooking process for the rice is complete, let it cool naturally until it reaches room temperature.
2. Take a bamboo sushi mat or a clean kitchen towel and position a sheet of nori seaweed on top of it.
3. Moisten your hands with water to avoid sticking, then take a generous handful of sushi rice. Gently and evenly distribute the rice over the nori sheet, ensuring to leave approximately 1 inch of empty space at the top.
4. Arrange your choice of vegetables in a line across the center of the rice.
5. Using the sushi mat or towel, tightly roll the nori sheet away from you, applying gentle pressure to keep the roll firm.
6. Dampen the upper edge of the nori sheet slightly by applying a small amount of water. This will help secure the roll together.
7. Continue the same procedure with the remaining nori sheets and ingredients, repeating the steps to create additional rolls.
8. After completing the preparation of all the rolls, utilize a sharp knife to carefully slice each roll into bite-sized pieces.
9. When serving the veggie sushi rolls, provide soy sauce as a dipping condiment. Additionally, you have the option to serve pickled ginger and wasabi on the side for added flavor and variety.

Nutritional breakdown per serving(1 roll): Calories: 150 kcal, Protein: 3 grams, Carbohydrates: 33 grams, Fat: 1 grams, Saturated Fat: 0 grams, Cholesterol: 0 milligrams, Sodium: 200 milligrams, Fiber: 2 grams, and Sugar: 1 grams.

CHAPTER 3:
SOUPS RECIPES

CLASSIC TOMATO SOUP

Prep Time: 10 minutes
Cooking Time: 30 minutes
Total Time: 40 minutes
Servings: 4

Ingredients:

- 4 tbsp of extra-virgin olive oil
- 5 tbsp butter, split
- 3 yellow onions, medium-sized, diced (approximately 3 cups)
- 3 large garlic cloves, minced
- 1/4 cup all-purpose flour
- 6 cups chicken broth
- 2 (28-ounce) cans whole peeled tomatoes
- 2 tablespoons sugar
- 1/2 teaspoon dried thyme
- Salt
- Freshly ground black pepper
- Fresh chopped basil, for serving (optional)
- Croutons, for serving (optional)
- Freshly grated Parmigiano-Reggiano, for serving (optional)

Directions:

1. Prepare for cooking by positioning a large pot on the stove over medium-low heat. In the pot, mix together the olive oil and 2 tablespoons of butter, and heat the combination until it reaches a warm temperature.
2. Introduce the chopped onions to the pot and cook them gently over low to medium heat. Stir occasionally as you cook until the onions become soft and translucent, which usually takes around 20 minutes.
3. After adding the minced garlic to the pot, ensure it is thoroughly mixed into the mixture. Continue cooking the mixture for an additional minute to further develop and enhance the overall flavor profile.
4. Sprinkle the all-purpose flour over the onions and garlic, stirring well to coat.
5. With caution, add the chicken broth to the pot, making sure to incorporate all the flour into the mixture. Stir the mixture thoroughly, ensuring that all the ingredients are fully combined.

6. To begin, carefully place the entire peeled tomatoes, along with their accompanying juice from the cans, into the pot. To ensure proper integration, gently break them up using either a spoon or spatula.
7. Stir in the sugar, dried thyme, salt, and freshly ground black pepper to taste.
8. Increase the heat slowly until the soup reaches a simmer. Let it cook for about 10 minutes, remembering to stir occasionally while it cooks.
9. When pureeing the soup to achieve a smooth and consistent texture, it is important to exercise caution whether you are using an immersion blender or a regular blender. This step should be done after removing the soup from the heat source. It is important to be mindful of the potential hazards involved in blending hot liquids.
10. Place the pot back on low heat and carefully incorporate the remaining 3 tablespoons of butter by stirring until it melts completely.
11. Sample the soup to evaluate its flavor and, if necessary, make adjustments to the seasoning to achieve the desired taste.
12. Ladle the classic tomato soup into bowls and garnish with fresh chopped basil, croutons, and freshly grated Parmigiano-Reggiano, if desired.
13. Serve hot and enjoy!

Nutritional breakdown per serving:

Calories: 330 kcal, Protein: 6 grams, Carbohydrates: 27 grams, Fat: 23 grams, Saturated Fat: 9 grams, Cholesterol: 5 milligrams, Sodium: 1100 milligrams, Fiber: 4 grams, and Sugar: 12 grams.

BUTTERNUT SQUASH SOUP

Prep Time: 15 minutes
Cooking Time: 30 minutes
Total Time: 45 minutes
Servings: 4

Ingredients:

- 1 medium-sized butternut squash (about 3 pounds)
- 1 tablespoon olive oil
- 1 medium onion, chopped
- 2 cloves garlic, minced
- 4 cups vegetable broth
- 1 teaspoon dried thyme
- 1/2 teaspoon ground cinnamon
- Salt and pepper, to taste
- Optional toppings: roasted pumpkin seeds, croutons, or a drizzle of cream

Directions:

1. Prior to initiating the cooking process, confirm that the oven has been preheated to 400°F (200°C).
2. To prepare the butternut squash, start by cutting it in half lengthwise. Remove the seeds and fibers from the center using a spoon. Next, brush the cut sides of the squash with olive oil. Finally, place the squash halves cut-side down on a baking sheet.
3. To cook the squash until it reaches a tender consistency, preheat the oven and place the squash inside. Roast it for approximately 40 minutes, or until the flesh becomes soft and can be easily pierced with a fork. After the squash is thoroughly cooked, remove it from the oven and let it cool slightly before proceeding.
4. As the squash roasts, it's time to create a flavorful onion and garlic mixture. Take a medium-sized pot and place it over medium heat. Proceed to heat the olive oil in the pot. Incorporate the finely chopped onion and minced garlic into the pot. Cook the mixture, periodically stirring, until the onion turns translucent and releases a delightful aroma.
5. Scoop out the roasted butternut squash flesh and add it to the pot with the onions and garlic. Stir well to combine.
6. After that, pour the vegetable broth into the pot and gently sprinkle in the dried thyme and ground cinnamon. Make sure all the ingredients are well combined by giving them a thorough mix. Next, adjust the seasoning to your preference by adding salt and pepper based on your personal taste.

7. After the mixture reaches a boiling point, reduce the heat and let it simmer for around 10 minutes. This gentle simmering will give the flavors enough time to harmoniously blend and meld together.
8. There are several methods available to help you achieve a smooth and creamy texture for your soup. One option is to use an immersion blender directly in the pot. If you prefer, you can also transfer the soup to a blender in smaller portions and blend it until it achieves a smooth and consistent texture.
9. Return the soup to the pot and heat it over low heat until warmed through.
10. Once the cooking process is complete, it is important to pause and sample the dish to ensure that the seasoning is to your liking. If necessary, make any required adjustments to enhance the flavor.
11. Ladle the butternut squash soup into bowls and garnish with roasted pumpkin seeds, croutons, or a drizzle of cream, if desired.
12. Serve hot and enjoy!

Nutritional breakdown per serving:

Calories: 180 kcal, Protein: 4 grams, Carbohydrates: 38 grams, Fat: 4 grams, Saturated Fat: 1 grams, Cholesterol: 0 milligrams, Sodium: 800 milligrams, Fiber: 4 grams, and Sugar: 10 grams.

LENTIL SOUP

Prep Time: 10 minutes
Cooking Time: 30 minutes
Total Time: 40 minutes
Servings: 4

Ingredients:

- 2 tablespoons olive oil
- 1 medium onion, chopped
- 2 cloves garlic, minced
- 2 carrots, diced
- 2 celery stalks, diced
- 1 cup dried red lentils
- 4 cups vegetable broth
- 1 bay leaf
- 1 teaspoon ground cumin
- 1/2 teaspoon paprika
- Salt and pepper, to taste
- Fresh parsley, for garnish (optional)
- Lemon wedges, for serving (optional)

Directions:

1. In order to warm up the olive oil, it should be placed in a large pot and heated over medium heat.
2. Combine the chopped onion and minced garlic in the pot, then sauté the mixture for 3-4 minutes until the onion becomes translucent.
3. Following that, add the diced carrots and celery to the pot. Continue cooking the mixture for an additional 3-4 minutes until the vegetables begin to soften.
4. Start by rinsing the red lentils under cold water, then proceed to add them to the pot.
5. Gently pour the vegetable broth into the pot, ensuring a steady and controlled stream. Next, incorporate the bay leaf, ground cumin, and paprika into the mixture.
6. To achieve the desired flavor, add salt and pepper to the dish according to your personal preference.
7. Once the mixture reaches a boiling point, lower the heat to a gentle simmer. Ensure the pot is covered and let the soup simmer for around 25 minutes, or until the lentils have achieved a tender texture.

8. Take out the bay leaf from the soup, ensuring it is completely removed before serving.
9. To reach the desired consistency, you can either use an immersion blender in the pot or transfer some of the soup to a blender. After blending until smooth, carefully pour the mixture back into the pot and give it a thorough stir.
10. Take a moment to taste the soup and make any necessary adjustments to the seasoning.
11. If you would like, you can serve the lentil soup in bowls and consider adding a garnish of fresh parsley.
12. If desired, you can serve the hot lentil soup with lemon wedges on the side, giving you the option to squeeze them over the soup according to your preference.

Nutritional breakdown per serving:

Calories: 250 kcal, Protein: 12 grams, Carbohydrates: 36 grams, Fat: 7 grams, Saturated Fat: 1 grams, Cholesterol: 0 milligrams, Sodium: 800 milligrams, Fiber: 15 grams, and Sugar: 6 grams.

MINESTRONE SOUP

Prep Time: 20 minutes
Cooking Time: 30 minutes
Total Time: 50 minutes
Servings: 6

Ingredients:

- 2 tablespoons olive oil
- 1 medium onion, chopped
- 2 cloves garlic, minced
- 2 carrots, diced
- 2 celery stalks, diced
- 1 medium zucchini, diced
- 1 cup of green beans into 1-inch pieces
- 1 can (14 ounces) diced tomatoes
- 4 cups vegetable broth
- 1 cup small pasta (e.g., macaroni, shells, or ditalini)
- 1 teaspoon dried basil
- 1 teaspoon dried oregano
- Salt and pepper, to taste
- Grated Parmesan cheese, for serving (optional)
- Fresh basil leaves, for garnish (optional)

Directions:

1. First, position a large pot on medium heat and then proceed to heat the olive oil.
2. After preparing the pot, incorporate the chopped onion and minced garlic, and then sauté them for approximately 3-4 minutes until the onion turns translucent.
3. Include the diced carrots, celery, zucchini, and green beans in the pot, and cook them for an extra 5 minutes while stirring occasionally.
4. Carefully pour the diced tomatoes, along with their juice, and the vegetable broth into the pot. Thoroughly stir the ingredients together.
5. Incorporate the small pasta, dried basil, dried oregano, salt, and pepper into the pot. Continuously heat the mixture until it reaches the boiling point.
6. Set the heat to a low simmer and allow the soup to simmer for approximately 15-20 minutes until the pasta and vegetables have become tender and cooked to your desired texture.

7. Sample the soup and make any necessary adjustments to the seasoning based on your taste preferences.
8. Scoop the minestrone soup into individual bowls. Serve it while hot, and for added flavor, you can optionally sprinkle grated Parmesan cheese on top and garnish with fresh basil leaves.

Nutritional breakdown per serving:

Calories: 220 kcal, Protein: 7 grams, Carbohydrates: 38 grams, Fat: 5 grams, Saturated Fat: 1 grams, Cholesterol: 0 milligrams, Sodium: 700 milligrams, Fiber: 7 grams, and Sugar: 7 grams.

CHICKEN NOODLE SOUP

Prep Time: 15 minutes
Cooking Time: 30 minutes
Total Time: 45 minutes
Servings: 4

Ingredients:

- 1 tablespoon olive oil
- 1 medium onion, diced
- 2 cloves garlic, minced
- 2 carrots, sliced
- 2 celery stalks, sliced
- 6 cups chicken broth
- 2 cups cooked chicken, shredded or diced
- 1 cup egg noodles
- 1 teaspoon dried thyme
- Salt and pepper, to taste
- Fresh parsley, for garnish (optional)

Directions:

1. To initiate the cooking process, start by warming the olive oil in a sizable pot over medium heat.
2. Incorporate the diced onion and minced garlic into the pot, then sauté them for approximately 2-3 minutes until the onion turns translucent.
3. Incorporate the sliced carrots and celery into the pot, and continue cooking for an additional 3-4 minutes until the vegetables begin to soften.
4. Proceed by adding the chicken broth to the pot and raising the heat until it reaches a boiling point.
5. Add the cooked chicken, egg noodles, dried thyme, salt, and pepper to the pot. Stir well.
6. Turn down the heat to a medium-low setting and let the soup gently simmer for around 10-15 minutes, or until the noodles have reached the desired level of doneness and the flavors have melded together into a delightful harmony.
7. If needed, sample the soup and make any necessary adjustments to the seasoning based on your personal preference.
8. Ladle the chicken noodle soup into bowls. Garnish with fresh parsley, if desired.
9. Serve hot and enjoy!

Nutritional breakdown per serving:

Calories: 250 kcal, Protein: 24 grams, Carbohydrates: 20 grams, Fat: 8 grams, Saturated Fat: 2 grams, Cholesterol: 35 milligrams, Sodium: 800 milligrams, Fiber: 2 grams, and Sugar: 3 grams.

POTATO LEEK SOUP

Prep Time: 15 minutes
Cooking Time: 30 minutes
Total Time: 45 minutes
Servings: 4

Ingredients:

- 2 tablespoons olive oil
- 2 leeks, white and light green parts only, sliced
- 3 cloves garlic, minced
- 4 medium potatoes, peeled and diced
- 4 cups vegetable broth
- 1 bay leaf
- 1 teaspoon dried thyme
- Salt and pepper, to taste
- Fresh chives, for garnish (optional)
- Crusty bread, for serving (optional)

Directions:

1. Exercise caution when heating the olive oil in a large pot over medium heat, ensuring it reaches the desired temperature with care.
2. Incorporate the sliced leeks into the pot and sauté them for approximately 5 minutes until they begin to soften.
3. Introduce the minced garlic and diced potatoes to the pot. Continuously stir and cook for an extra 3 minutes.
4. Gently pour the vegetable broth into the pot and include the bay leaf and dried thyme. Season with salt and pepper to taste.
5. After the liquid in the pot begins to boil, lower the heat to a gentle flame. Make sure to tightly cover the pot and let the soup simmer softly for approximately 20 minutes, or until the potatoes have achieved a tender texture.
6. Before serving the soup, make sure to remove and dispose of the bay leaf.
7. To obtain the desired thickness, there are two options. Firstly, you can use an immersion blender directly in the pot. Another option is to transfer a portion of the soup to a blender and blend it until the desired texture is achieved. Once done, pour the blended soup back into the pot and mix it well.
8. Sample the soup and make any necessary adjustments to the seasoning according to your taste.
9. Ladle the potato leek soup into bowls. Garnish with fresh chives, if desired.

10. If desired, serve the soup hot and accompany it with a side of crusty bread.

Nutritional breakdown per serving:

Calories: 250 kcal, Protein: 5 grams, Carbohydrates: 42 grams, Fat: 7 grams, Saturated Fat: 1 grams, Cholesterol: 0 milligrams, Sodium: 800 milligrams, Fiber: 5 grams, and Sugar: 4 grams.

CREAMY MUSHROOM SOUP

Cooking Time: 30 minutes

Total Time: 45 minutes

Servings: 4

Ingredients:

- 2 tablespoons olive oil
- 1 medium onion, diced
- 2 cloves garlic, minced
- 1 pound mushrooms, sliced
- 4 cups vegetable broth
- 1 cup heavy cream
- 1 teaspoon dried thyme
- Salt and pepper, to taste
- Fresh parsley, for garnish (optional)

Directions:

1. Start by placing a generously-sized pot on the stove. Allow the pot to heat up as you pour in a drizzle of olive oil. Adjust the heat to medium and let the oil gradually warm up.
2. Combine the diced onion and minced garlic in the pot, then sauté the mixture for approximately 2-3 minutes until the onion becomes translucent.
3. Incorporate the sliced mushrooms into the pot and let them cook for roughly 5 minutes until they release their moisture and achieve a desirable brown hue.
4. Once the vegetable broth has been added to the pot, heat it until it reaches a boiling point. Subsequently, reduce the heat to a gentle simmer and allow the mixture to cook for a duration of 10 minutes.
5. In order to achieve the desired consistency, you can choose between using an immersion blender directly in the pot or transferring a portion of the soup to a blender. After blending the soup to your desired texture, carefully transfer it back into the pot.
6. After incorporating the heavy cream and dried thyme into the pot, ensure thorough stirring to combine them with the mixture. Take the opportunity to season the mixture with salt and pepper, making adjustments based on your individual taste preferences.
7. Allow the soup to simmer for an extra 5 minutes, ensuring that it heats through.
8. Pause to taste the soup and make any required seasoning adjustments based on your personal preference.

9. Ladle the creamy mushroom soup into bowls. Garnish with fresh parsley, if desired.
10. Serve hot and enjoy!

Nutritional breakdown per serving:

Calories: 280 kcal, Protein: 5 grams, Carbohydrates: 12 grams, Fat: 24 grams, Saturated Fat: 12 grams, Cholesterol: 50 milligrams, Sodium: 800 milligrams, Fiber: 2 grams, and Sugar: 5 grams.

TORTILLA SOUP

Prep Time: 15 minutes
Cooking Time: 30 minutes
Total Time: 45 minutes
Servings: 4

Ingredients:

- 2 tablespoons olive oil
- 1 medium onion, diced
- 2 cloves garlic, minced
- 1 jalapeño pepper, seeded and finely chopped
- 1 red bell pepper, diced
- 1 teaspoon ground cumin
- 1 teaspoon chili powder
- 4 cups vegetable broth
- 1 can (14 ounces) diced tomatoes
- 1 cup corn kernels (fresh or frozen)
- 1 cup black beans, rinsed and drained
- 1 cup cooked shredded chicken
- 1/2 cup heavy cream
- Salt and pepper, to taste
- Tortilla chips, for serving
- Shredded cheese, for serving
- Fresh cilantro, for garnish (optional)
- Lime wedges, for serving (optional)

Directions:

1. Begin by selecting a generously-sized pot and placing it on the stove. Drizzle a small amount of olive oil into the pot, then adjust the heat to medium and allow the oil to gradually warm up.
2. Combine the diced onion, minced garlic, jalapeño pepper, and red bell pepper in a pot. Sauté the mixture over medium heat for approximately 5 minutes, or until the vegetables begin to soften.
3. After combining the diced onion, minced garlic, jalapeño pepper, and red bell pepper in the pot, proceed to stir in the ground cumin and chili powder. Cook the mixture for an additional minute to allow the spices to toast.

4. Add the vegetable broth and diced tomatoes (including their juice) to the pot. Bring the mixture to a boil.
5. Reduce the heat to low and add the corn kernels, black beans, and shredded chicken to the pot. Let the mixture simmer for a period of 15 minutes, allowing the flavors to blend harmoniously.
6. After the 15-minute simmering period, it is time to incorporate the heavy cream into the mixture. Take the opportunity to season it with salt and pepper according to your taste. Extend the cooking time of the mixture by an additional 5 minutes to enhance the development of flavors.
7. Ladle the creamy tortilla soup into bowls. Serve with tortilla chips, shredded cheese, fresh cilantro, and lime wedges on the side for garnish and added flavor.
8. Enjoy while hot!

Nutritional breakdown per serving:

Calories: 380 kcal, Protein: 18 grams, Carbohydrates: 35 grams, Fat: 20 grams, Saturated Fat: 8 grams, Cholesterol: 0 milligrams, Sodium: 900 milligrams, Fiber: 7 grams, and Sugar: 7 grams.

THAI COCONUT CURRY SOUP

Prep Time: 20 minutes
Cooking Time: 30 minutes
Total Time: 50 minutes
Servings: 4

Ingredients:

- 2 tablespoons olive oil
- 1 medium onion, diced
- 2 cloves garlic, minced
- 1 jalapeño pepper, seeded and finely chopped
- 1 red bell pepper, diced
- 1 teaspoon ground cumin
- 1 teaspoon chili powder
- 4 cups vegetable broth
- 1 can (14 ounces) coconut milk
- 2 tablespoons Thai red curry paste
- 1 tablespoon reduced-sodium tamari (or soy sauce)
- 1 teaspoon lime zest
- 2 tablespoons lime juice
- 1/2 teaspoon salt
- 2 cups mixed vegetables (such as sliced mushrooms, bell peppers, and snow peas)
- 1 cup cooked protein (such as diced chicken, shrimp, or tofu)
- Fresh cilantro, for garnish (optional)
- Lime wedges, for serving (optional)

Directions:

1. Begin by selecting a generously-sized pot and placing it on the stove. Drizzle a small amount of olive oil into the pot, then adjust the heat to medium and allow the oil to gradually warm up.
2. Add the diced onion, minced garlic, jalapeño pepper, and red bell pepper to the pot. Sauté for 5 minutes until the vegetables start to soften.
3. Blend the ground cumin and chili powder into the mixture, stirring well. Let the spices cook for an extra minute, utilizing a technique called toasting. This process enhances the spices' aromas and flavors, resulting in a more delightful culinary experience.

4. Incorporate the vegetable broth and coconut milk into the mixture by pouring them in. Stir in the Thai red curry paste, reduced-sodium tamari, lime zest, lime juice, and salt. Bring the mixture to a boil.
5. After reducing the heat to a gentle simmer, carefully add the mixed vegetables and cooked protein to the pot, making sure they are thoroughly mixed in. Leave the mixture to simmer for a duration of 10 to 15 minutes, enabling the vegetables to achieve a tender texture and the flavors to harmoniously meld together.
6. Sample the soup and modify the seasoning as necessary to achieve the desired taste.
7. Using a ladle, carefully portion the Thai coconut curry soup into individual bowls. Optionally, garnish with fresh cilantro to add a burst of flavor. Serve the soup alongside lime wedges, allowing diners to squeeze them over the soup according to their preference.
8. Enjoy while hot!

Nutritional breakdown per serving:

Calories: 280 kcal, Protein: 6 grams, Carbohydrates: 20 grams, Fat: 20 grams, Saturated Fat: 14 grams, Cholesterol: 0 milligrams, Sodium: 900 milligrams, Fiber: 4 grams, and Sugar: 6 grams.

BROCCOLI CHEDDAR SOUP

Cooking Time: 30 minutes

Total Time: 45 minutes

Servings: 4

Ingredients:

- 2 tablespoons olive oil
- 1 medium onion, diced
- 2 cloves garlic, minced
- 1 jalapeño pepper, seeded and finely chopped (optional)
- 1 red bell pepper, diced
- 1 teaspoon ground cumin
- 1 teaspoon chili powder
- 4 cups vegetable broth
- 1 can (14 ounces) coconut milk
- 2 tablespoons Thai red curry paste
- 1 tablespoon reduced-sodium tamari (or soy sauce)
- 1 teaspoon lime zest
- 2 tablespoons lime juice
- 1/2 teaspoon salt
- 2 cups mixed vegetables (such as sliced mushrooms, bell peppers, and snow peas)
- 1 cup cooked protein (such as diced chicken, shrimp, or tofu)
- Fresh cilantro, for garnish (optional)
- Lime wedges, for serving (optional)

Directions:

1. To start, choose a pot that provides ample space and position it on the stove. Add a modest drizzle of olive oil to the pot, then set the heat to medium and let the oil gradually heat up.
2. Add the diced onion, minced garlic, jalapeño pepper (if using), and red bell pepper to the pot. Sauté for 5 minutes until the vegetables start to soften.
3. Incorporate the ground cumin and chili powder into the mixture by stirring them in. Continue cooking the mixture for an extra minute to allow the spices to toast and release their flavors.
4. Introduce the vegetable broth and coconut milk into the mixture by pouring them in. Stir in the Thai red curry paste, reduced-sodium tamari, lime zest, lime juice, and salt. Bring the mixture to a boil.

5. Once the heat has been reduced to a low setting, carefully add the mixed vegetables and cooked protein to the pot. Allow the mixture to simmer for a period of 10 to 15 minutes until the vegetables reach a tender state and the flavors have harmoniously melded together.
6. Sample the soup and, if necessary, make adjustments to the seasoning according to your taste preferences.
7. Using a ladle, carefully transfer the Thai coconut curry soup into individual bowls. Optionally, enhance the presentation by garnishing with fresh cilantro. Additionally, provide lime wedges on the side, allowing diners to squeeze them over the soup for added tanginess, if desired.
8. Enjoy while hot!

Nutritional breakdown per serving:

Calories: 280 kcal, Protein: 6 grams, Carbohydrates: 20 grams, Fat: 20 grams, Saturated Fat: 14 grams, Cholesterol: 30 milligrams, Sodium: 900 milligrams, Fiber: 4 grams, and Sugar: 6 grams.

ITALIAN WEDDING SOUP

Prep Time: 20 minutes
Cooking Time: 30 minutes
Total Time: 50 minutes
Servings: 4

Ingredients:

- 1 tablespoon olive oil
- 1 small onion, finely chopped
- 2 cloves garlic, minced
- 2 carrots, diced
- 2 celery stalks, diced
- 4 cups chicken broth
- 1 cup small pasta
- 1 cup cooked meatballs, homemade or store-bought
- 2 cups fresh spinach, chopped
- Salt and pepper, to taste
- Grated Parmesan cheese, for serving

Directions:

1. Begin by selecting a pot that offers sufficient room and place it on the stovetop. Drizzle a small amount of olive oil into the pot, then adjust the heat to medium and allow the oil to slowly heat up.
2. Add the chopped onion, minced garlic, diced carrots, and diced celery to the pot. Sauté for 5 minutes until the vegetables start to soften.
3. Incorporate the chicken broth into the pot and heat it until it reaches a rapid boil.
4. Place the small pasta into the pot and adhere to the instructions on the package for cooking, ensuring that it reaches the desired al dente texture.
5. Stir in the cooked meatballs and chopped spinach. Cook for an additional 5 minutes until the spinach wilts.
6. Personalize the flavor of the soup by modifying the seasoning to match your taste. Incorporate salt and pepper based on your preferences, ensuring that the soup is seasoned to your liking.
7. Ladle the Italian wedding soup into bowls. Serve hot, garnished with grated Parmesan cheese.

Nutritional breakdown per serving:

Calories: 320 kcal, Protein: 20 grams, Carbohydrates: 32 grams, Fat: 12 grams, Saturated Fat: 4 grams, Cholesterol: 21 milligrams, Sodium: 900 milligrams, Fiber: 4 grams, and Sugar: 5 grams.

CORN CHOWDER

Prep Time: 15 minutes
Cooking Time: 30 minutes
Total Time: 45 minutes
Servings: 4

Ingredients:

- 2 tablespoons butter
- 1 medium onion, diced
- 2 cloves garlic, minced
- 4 cups fresh or frozen corn kernels
- 2 medium potatoes, peeled and diced
- 4 cups vegetable or chicken broth
- 1 cup milk
- 1 cup heavy cream
- 1 teaspoon dried thyme
- Salt and pepper, to taste
- Chopped fresh parsley, for garnish (optional)

Directions:

1. To start, choose an adequately sized pot and position it on the stovetop. Add a modest amount of olive oil to the pot, ensuring it is evenly distributed. Proceed to adjust the heat to a medium setting, allowing the oil to gradually heat up.
2. Incorporate the diced onion and minced garlic into the pot, ensuring they are evenly distributed. Sauté the mixture for approximately 5 minutes, or until the onion turns translucent.
3. Include the corn kernels and diced potatoes into the pot. Stir the mixture and continue cooking for an additional 5 minutes.
4. Carefully distribute the vegetable or chicken broth into the pot, making sure it is evenly poured throughout. After the mixture has come to a boil, adjust the heat to a gentle simmer and allow it to cook for around 15 minutes, or until the potatoes have become tender.
5. To achieve the desired consistency, you have two options. Firstly, you can utilize an immersion blender directly in the pot. In case you prefer an alternative method, you can choose to transfer a portion of the soup to a blender. Proceed to blend the soup until it attains the desired texture, and then meticulously pour it back into the pot.

6. Incorporate the milk, heavy cream, dried thyme, salt, and pepper into the mixture, ensuring they are well combined. Continue to let the mixture simmer for an extra 5 minutes to ensure that it is heated thoroughly.
7. Sample the soup and, if necessary, make adjustments to the seasoning according to your taste preferences.
8. Ladle the creamy corn chowder into bowls. Garnish with chopped fresh parsley, if desired.
9. Serve hot and enjoy!

Nutritional breakdown per serving:

Calories: 380 kcal, Protein: 8 grams, Carbohydrates: 42 grams, Fat: 22 grams, Saturated Fat: 14 grams, Cholesterol: 20 milligrams, Sodium: 800 milligrams, Fiber: 5 grams, and Sugar: 9 grams.

BLACK BEAN SOUP

Prep Time: 15 minutes
Cooking Time: 30 minutes
Total Time: 45 minutes
Servings: 4

Ingredients:

- 2 tablespoons olive oil
- 1 medium onion, diced
- 2 cloves garlic, minced
- 2 cans (15 ounces each) black beans, drained and rinsed
- 1 can (14.5 ounces) diced tomatoes
- 2 cups vegetable broth
- 1 teaspoon ground cumin
- 1 teaspoon chili powder
- 1/2 teaspoon smoked paprika
- Salt and pepper, to taste
- 1/4 cup chopped fresh cilantro, for garnish
- Optional serving: Sour cream or Greek yogurt
- Lime wedges, for serving (optional)

Directions:

1. Begin by placing a large pot on the stove. Set the heat to medium and allow the pot to warm up. Once the pot is heated, add the olive oil and let it heat up as well.
2. Once the pot is ready with the heated olive oil, introduce the diced onion and minced garlic into the mix. Allow them to sauté for approximately 5 minutes, or until the onion turns translucent, indicating its softness and enhanced flavors.
3. Add the black beans, diced tomatoes (with their juice), vegetable broth, ground cumin, chili powder, smoked paprika, salt, and pepper to the pot. Stir well to combine.
4. After the mixture boils, lower the heat to a gentle simmer and let it cook for approximately 20 minutes. This allows the flavors to blend harmoniously, resulting in a delightful combination. The simmering process enhances the taste, resulting in a rich and well-rounded flavor profile.
5. To achieve the desired balance between thickness and texture, utilize either an immersion blender or a regular blender. This will help in blending the ingredients

together smoothly. Blend approximately half of the soup until it becomes smooth and velvety, effectively thickening the soup while maintaining a pleasing texture.

6. After blending the soup, pour it back into the pot and give it a thorough stir.
7. Sample the soup and make any necessary adjustments to the seasoning.
8. Carefully pour the creamy black bean soup into bowls and sprinkle with fresh cilantro for added fragrance. For extra flavor, top with a dollop of sour cream or Greek yogurt. Serve with lime wedges on the side to add a tangy taste.
9. Enjoy while hot!

Nutritional breakdown per serving:

Calories: 220 kcal, Protein: 11 grams, Carbohydrates: 34 grams, Fat: 6 grams, Saturated Fat: 1 grams, Cholesterol: 2 milligrams, Sodium: 800 milligrams, Fiber: 12 grams, and Sugar: 4 grams.

CREAMY CAULIFLOWER SOUP

Prep Time: 15 minutes
Cooking Time: 30 minutes
Total Time: 45 minutes
Servings: 4

Ingredients:

- 2 tablespoons olive oil
- 1 medium onion, chopped
- 2 cloves garlic, minced
- 1 large head cauliflower, cut into florets
- 4 cups vegetable broth
- 1 cup milk (or plant-based milk for a vegan option)
- Salt and pepper, to taste
- Fresh parsley, for garnish (optional)

Directions:

1. Begin by preparing a large pot on the stove and adjusting the heat to medium. Proceed to add the olive oil to the pot and let it heat up accordingly.
2. Incorporate the chopped onion and minced garlic into the pot, ensuring they are evenly distributed. Sauté the mixture for approximately 5 minutes, or until the onion achieves a translucent appearance.
3. Let the cauliflower florets cook in the pot for an extra 5 minutes, remembering to stir occasionally to ensure even cooking.
4. Incorporate the vegetable broth into the pot and bring it to a boiling point. Reduce the heat to a gentle simmer and let the mixture simmer for around 15 to 20 minutes until the cauliflower reaches a tender texture, making sure it attains the desired consistency.
5. To achieve a smooth and creamy consistency, there are two methods you can employ. The first option is to utilize an immersion blender. If you prefer, you have the option to transfer the soup into a traditional blender and blend it until it achieves the desired texture.
6. After blending the soup, pour it back into the pot and incorporate the milk. Proceed to gently warm the soup over low heat until it is thoroughly heated.
7. Customize the seasoning of the soup by adding salt and pepper to suit your individual taste.
8. Ladle the creamy cauliflower soup into bowls. Garnish with fresh parsley, if desired.
9. Serve hot and enjoy!

Nutritional breakdown per serving:

Calories: 150 kcal, Protein: 6 grams, Carbohydrates: 16 grams, Fat: 8 grams, Saturated Fat: 1 grams, Cholesterol: 0 milligrams, Sodium: 800 milligrams, Fiber: 5 grams, and Sugar: 7 grams.

MOROCCAN LENTIL SOUP

Prep Time: 15 minutes

Cooking Time: 30 minutes

Total Time: 45 minutes

Servings: 4

Ingredients:

- 2 tablespoons olive oil
- 1 medium onion, finely chopped
- 2 cloves garlic, minced
- 1 teaspoon ground cumin
- 1 teaspoon ground ginger
- 1 teaspoon ground cinnamon
- 1/2 teaspoon ground turmeric
- 1/4 teaspoon cayenne pepper (optional, for heat)
- 1 cup red lentils, rinsed
- 4 cups vegetable broth
- 1 can (14.5 ounces) diced tomatoes
- 1 cup chopped carrots
- 1 cup chopped potatoes
- Salt and pepper, to taste
- Fresh cilantro, for garnish (optional)

Directions:

1. To guarantee the desired level of heating, add a generous quantity of olive oil to the pot and heat it over medium heat.
2. Start by adding the chopped onion and minced garlic to the pot. Sauté the mixture for 5 minutes, or until the onion turns translucent.
3. Next, stir in the ground cumin, ground ginger, ground cinnamon, ground turmeric, and cayenne pepper (if desired). Let the spices cook for an extra minute to toast them, enhancing their flavors.
4. Add the red lentils, vegetable broth, diced tomatoes (with their juice), chopped carrots, and chopped potatoes to the pot. Stir well to combine.
5. Once the mixture reaches a boiling point, reduce the heat to a gentle simmer. Proceed by covering the pot and allowing it to simmer for a duration of 20-25 minutes until the lentils and vegetables have attained a tender consistency.

6. Customize the flavor of the mixture by incorporating salt and pepper to match your individual taste preferences.
7. Ladle the Moroccan lentil soup into bowls. Garnish with fresh cilantro, if desired.
8. Serve hot and enjoy!

Nutritional breakdown per serving:

Calories: 280 kcal, Protein: 14 grams, Carbohydrates: 44 grams, Fat: 7 grams, Saturated Fat: 1 grams, Cholesterol: 0 milligrams, Sodium: 800 milligrams, Fiber: 15 grams, and Sugar: 6 grams.

CHAPTER 4: PIZZA AND PASTA RECIPES

MARGHERITA PIZZA

Prep Time: 15 minutes
Cooking Time: 7 minutes
Total Time: 22 minutes
Servings: 4 (2 slices each)

Ingredients:

- 1 can (14 ounces) of crushed tomatoes, preferably San Marzano
- 3 medium garlic cloves, minced
- 1/2 teaspoon salt
- 1/2 teaspoon sugar
- 1/2 teaspoon freshly ground black pepper
- 2 tablespoons extra-virgin olive oil
- 1 (12-inch) round of pizza dough, stretched
- 2 ounces fresh mozzarella, thinly sliced
- Fresh basil leaves, for garnish

Directions:

1. Preheat your oven to its maximum temperature, typically ranging from 500 to 550 degrees Fahrenheit.
2. In a small bowl, mix together the crushed tomatoes, minced garlic, salt, sugar, black pepper, and olive oil to make the tomato sauce.
3. Move the stretched pizza dough onto a baking sheet or pizza stone.
4. Evenly distribute the tomato sauce on the dough, ensuring to leave a small border around the edges.
5. Arrange the thinly sliced mozzarella on top of the sauce.
6. Once you've preheated the oven, carefully place the pizza inside and bake it until the crust achieves a delightful golden brown color and the cheese has melted and lightly browned. This process usually takes approximately 7 minutes.
7. After taking the pizza out of the oven, allow it to cool for a brief period, around a minute or two.
8. Garnish with fresh basil leaves.
9. Slice the pizza into triangular wedges and serve it promptly.

Nutritional breakdown per serving(2 slices):

Calories: 320 kcal, Protein: 9 grams, Carbohydrates: 45 grams, Fat: 12 grams, Saturated Fat: 3 grams, Cholesterol: 0 milligrams, Sodium: 650 milligrams, Fiber: 3 grams, and Sugar: 4 grams.

VEGGIE SUPREME PIZZA

Prep Time: 15 minutes
Cooking Time: 12-15 minutes
Total Time: 27-30 minutes
Servings: 4 (1 pizza)

Ingredients:

- 1 pizza dough (store-bought or homemade)
- 1/2 cup marinara sauce
- 1 cup of mozzarella cheese, shredded
- 1/2 cup sliced bell peppers
- 1/2 cup sliced red onion
- 1/2 cup sliced mushrooms
- 1/4 cup sliced black olives
- 1/4 cup sliced cherry tomatoes
- 1/4 cup sliced artichoke hearts
- 1/4 teaspoon dried oregano
- 1/4 teaspoon dried basil
- Salt and pepper, to taste
- Fresh basil leaves, for garnish (optional)

Directions:

1. Before you begin, ensure that your oven is preheated to the temperature specified on the pizza dough packaging, or to 475°F (245°C) if you are using homemade dough.
2. Take the pizza dough and flatten it on a surface dusted lightly with flour until it reaches the desired thickness.
3. Gently transfer the flattened dough onto a pizza stone or baking sheet with caution.
4. Evenly distribute the marinara sauce across the dough, making sure to leave a small border around the edges.
5. Evenly distribute the marinara sauce over the dough, ensuring to leave a small border around the edges.
6. Arrange the sliced bell peppers, red onion, mushrooms, black olives, cherry tomatoes, and artichoke hearts on top of the cheese.
7. Sprinkle the dried oregano, dried basil, salt, and pepper over the toppings.
8. To cook the pizza, simply place it in the oven that has been preheated. Allow it to cook for approximately 12-15 minutes, or until the crust turns a beautiful golden color and the cheese melts and starts to bubble.

9. Once the pizza is done cooking, handle it with care and remove it from the oven. Give it a short cooling period, typically lasting around one to two minutes, before serving or cutting into it.
10. Garnish with fresh basil leaves, if desired.
11. To serve the pizza, cut it into triangular wedges and serve while it is still hot.

Nutritional breakdown per serving(1/4 of the pizza):

Calories: 280 kcal, Protein: 11 grams, Carbohydrates: 39 grams, Fat: 9 grams, Saturated Fat: 4 grams, Cholesterol: 0 milligrams, Sodium: 600 milligrams, Fiber: 3 grams, and Sugar: 4 grams.

BBQ CHICKEN PIZZA

Prep Time: 2 hours, 10 minutes (includes dough rising)
Cooking Time: 15 minutes
Total Time: 2 hours, 25 minutes
Servings: 1 (12-inch pizza)

Ingredients:

For the pizza dough:

- 2 1/4 teaspoons (1 packet) active dry yeast
- 1 teaspoon sugar
- 3/4 cup warm water
- 2 cups all-purpose flour
- 1 teaspoon salt
- 2 tablespoons olive oil

For the toppings:

- 1/2 cup BBQ sauce
- 1 cup cooked chicken breast, shredded
- 1/4 cup red onion, thinly sliced
- 1 cup shredded mozzarella cheese
- Fresh cilantro, chopped (optional)

Directions:

1. To begin, gather a small bowl for the mixing process. In this bowl, you will combine the active dry yeast, sugar, and warm water. This step is crucial for activating the yeast and kickstarting the fermentation process. Let it sit for 5 minutes until the mixture becomes frothy.
2. In a large mixing bowl, whisk together the all-purpose flour and salt. Make a well in the center and pour in the yeast mixture and olive oil.
3. Combine the ingredients thoroughly until they come together to form a cohesive dough. Then, transfer the dough onto a surface that has been lightly dusted with flour. To achieve a smooth and elastic consistency, dedicate about 5 minutes to kneading the dough.
4. Prepare a greased bowl and carefully transfer the dough into it, taking care to place it properly. Allow the bowl to rest in a warm area for approximately 1-2 hours, with a

clean kitchen towel placed over it. Over this period, the dough will undergo rising and double in size.

5. Before you proceed, ensure that your oven is preheated to its maximum temperature, typically ranging from 500 to 550 degrees Fahrenheit.

6. After allowing the dough to rise, release the air by gently punching it down. Next, transfer the deflated dough to a floured surface. Roll it out into a round shape with a diameter of approximately 12 inches.

7. Transfer the dough that has been rolled out onto a pizza stone or baking sheet with caution.

8. Evenly distribute the **BBQ** sauce over the dough, making sure to leave a small border around the edges.

9. Distribute the shredded chicken, red onion, and shredded mozzarella cheese evenly over the sauce.

10. Place the pizza in the oven that has been preheated and bake it for approximately 12-15 minutes. Monitor its progress closely and take it out of the oven as soon as the crust has turned golden and the cheese has melted and become bubbly.

11. Give the pizza a brief cooling period of approximately one to two minutes after taking it out of the oven.

12. Garnish with fresh cilantro, if desired.

13. Slice the pizza and serve hot.

Nutritional breakdown per serving (1/4 of the pizza):

Calories: 450 kcal, Protein: 22 grams, Carbohydrates: 60 grams, Fat: 14 grams, Saturated Fat: 5 grams, Cholesterol: 0 milligrams, Sodium: 950 milligrams, Fiber: 3 grams, and Sugar: 18 grams.

PESTO AND TOMATO PIZZA

rep Time: 20 minutes (includes making pesto)
Cooking Time: 12-15 minutes
Total Time: 32-35 minutes
Servings: 4 (1 pizza)

Ingredients:

For the pizza dough:

- 1 lb. pizza dough (store-bought or homemade)
- 2 tablespoons olive oil

For the pesto:

- 1 cup packed fresh basil leaves
- 1/4 cup pine nuts, lightly toasted
- 2 cloves garlic
- 1/4 cup grated Parmesan cheese
- 1/4 cup extra-virgin olive oil
- Salt and pepper, to taste

For the toppings:

- 1/2 cup pesto sauce
- 1 large tomato, sliced
- 1 cup shredded mozzarella cheese
- Fresh basil leaves, for garnish (optional)

Directions:

1. To begin, ensure that your oven is preheated to its maximum temperature, typically ranging from 500 to 550 degrees Fahrenheit.
2. Take the pizza dough and roll it out on a surface that has been lightly dusted with flour until it reaches the desired thickness
3. Move the rolled-out dough carefully onto a pizza stone or baking sheet, ensuring to handle it with care.
4. Brush the entire crust with olive oil.

5. In a food processor, combine the fresh basil leaves, toasted pine nuts, garlic, grated Parmesan cheese, and extra-virgin olive oil. Process until smooth. Season with salt and pepper to taste.
6. Evenly distribute the pesto sauce over the dough, making sure to leave a small border around the edges for a well-balanced flavor.
7. Place the sliced tomatoes on the pesto sauce, arranging them in an even manner.
8. Ensure complete coverage by sprinkling the shredded mozzarella cheese evenly over the sliced tomatoes.
9. Once the pizza is in the preheated oven, let it bake for approximately 12-15 minutes, or until the crust reaches a golden color and the cheese melts and starts to bubble.
10. Take the pizza out of the oven and allow it to cool for a short period, typically around one to two minutes.
11. Garnish with fresh basil leaves, if desired.
12. Slice the pizza and serve hot.

Nutritional breakdown per serving(1/4 of the pizza):

Calories: 450 kcal, Protein: 14 grams, Carbohydrates: 42 grams, Fat: 25 grams, Saturated Fat: 6 grams, Cholesterol: 0 milligrams, Sodium: 600 milligrams, Fiber: 2 grams, and Sugar: 3 grams.

SPINACH AND MUSHROOM PIZZA

Prep Time: 20 minutes
Cooking Time: 12-15 minutes
Total Time: 32-35 minutes
Servings: 4 (1 pizza)

Ingredients:

- 1 lb. pizza dough (store-bought or homemade)
- 2 tablespoons olive oil
- 1/2 cup pizza sauce or marinara sauce
- 1 1/2 cups shredded mozzarella cheese
- 1 cup sliced mushrooms
- 1 cup fresh spinach leaves
- 1/4 cup sliced black olives (optional)
- 1/4 teaspoon dried oregano
- Salt and pepper, to taste

Directions:

1. Ensure that your oven is preheated to its highest temperature, typically ranging from 500 to 550 degrees Fahrenheit, before you start.
2. Take the pizza dough and roll it out on a surface that has been lightly dusted with flour until it reaches the desired thickness.
3. Carefully move the rolled-out dough onto a pizza stone or baking sheet.
4. Brush the entire crust with olive oil.
5. Evenly distribute the pizza sauce or marinara sauce over the dough, making sure to leave a small border around the edges.
6. Evenly distribute the shredded mozzarella cheese on top of the sauce, ensuring it covers the surface.
7. Arrange the sliced mushrooms, fresh spinach leaves, and black olives (if using) on top of the cheese.
8. Evenly distribute the dried oregano, salt, and pepper over the toppings, ensuring they are spread out evenly.
9. Once the pizza is in the preheated oven, let it bake for approximately 12-15 minutes, or until the crust reaches a golden color and the cheese melts and starts to bubble.
10. Give the pizza a brief cooling period of approximately one to two minutes after taking it out of the oven.
11. Slice the pizza and serve hot.

Nutritional breakdown per serving(1/4 of the pizza):

Calories: 320 kcal, Protein: 14 grams, Carbohydrates: 40 grams, Fat: 12 grams, Saturated Fat: 4 grams, Cholesterol: 0 milligrams, Sodium: 600 milligrams, Fiber: 3 grams, and Sugar: 3 grams.

MEDITERRANEAN PIZZA

Prep Time: 20 minutes
Cooking Time: 12-15 minutes
Total Time: 32-35 minutes
Servings: 4 (1 pizza)

Ingredients:

- 1 lb. pizza dough (store-bought or homemade)
- 2 tablespoons olive oil
- 1/2 cup pizza sauce or marinara sauce
- 1 1/2 cups shredded mozzarella cheese
- 1 cup sliced mushrooms
- 1 cup fresh spinach leaves
- 1/4 cup sliced black olives (optional)
- 1/4 teaspoon dried oregano
- Salt and pepper, to taste

Directions:

1. Before you start, make sure to preheat your oven to its maximum temperature, usually between 500 to 550 degrees Fahrenheit.
2. Roll out the pizza dough on a surface that has been lightly dusted with flour until it reaches your desired thickness.
3. Move the rolled-out dough carefully onto a pizza stone or baking sheet, ensuring to handle it with care.
4. Brush the entire crust with olive oil.
5. Evenly distribute the pizza sauce or marinara sauce over the dough, making sure to leave a small border around the edges.
6. Evenly distribute the shredded mozzarella cheese on top of the sauce, ensuring it covers the surface.
7. Arrange the sliced mushrooms, fresh spinach leaves, and black olives (if using) on top of the cheese.
8. Evenly distribute the dried oregano, salt, and pepper over the toppings, ensuring they are spread out evenly.
9. Once the pizza is in the preheated oven, let it bake for approximately 12-15 minutes, or until the crust reaches a golden color and the cheese melts and starts to bubble.
10. Take the pizza out of the oven and allow it to cool for a short period, typically around one to two minutes.
11. Slice the pizza and serve hot.

Nutritional breakdown per serving:

Calories: 320 kcal, Protein: 14 grams, Carbohydrates: 40 grams, Fat: 12 grams, Saturated Fat: 4 grams, Cholesterol: 0 milligrams, Sodium: 600 milligrams, Fiber: 3 grams, and Sugar: 3 grams.

CLASSIC SPAGHETTI AGLIO E OLIO

Prep Time: 10 minutes
Cooking Time: 15 minutes
Total Time: 25 minutes
Servings: 4

Ingredients:

- 1 lb. spaghetti
- 1/2 cup extra-virgin olive oil
- 6 cloves garlic, thinly sliced
- 1/2 teaspoon red pepper flakes (adjust to taste)
- Salt, to taste
- Fresh parsley, chopped (optional)

Directions:

1. To start, fill a large pot with water and add a generous amount of salt. Bring the water to a boil. Next, proceed to cook the spaghetti following the guidelines provided on the package until it reaches the desired al dente texture. Before proceeding to drain the spaghetti, it is important to remember to reserve 1/2 cup of the pasta cooking water for later use.
2. While the pasta cooks, heat olive oil in a skillet over medium heat. Sauté the garlic and red pepper flakes in the skillet, stirring regularly, until the garlic turns golden brown and releases a fragrant aroma. This process typically takes about 2-3 minutes.
3. After removing the skillet from the heat, place the cooked pasta into the skillet. Coat the pasta thoroughly in the garlic-infused oil by tossing it. If the pasta appears dry, gradually add small amounts of the reserved pasta cooking water until you achieve the desired consistency.
4. Season the pasta with salt to your liking and toss it once more to ensure proper blending.
5. Serve the spaghetti aglio e olio hot, garnished with fresh parsley if desired.

Nutritional breakdown per serving(1/4 of the recipe):

Calories: 550 kcal, Protein: 11 grams, Carbohydrates: 65 grams, Fat: 27 grams, Saturated Fat: 4 grams, Cholesterol: 0 milligrams, Sodium: 300 milligrams, Fiber: 3 grams, and Sugar: 2 grams.

CREAMY VEGAN ALFREDO

Prep Time: 10 minutes
Cooking Time: 15 minutes
Total Time: 25 minutes
Servings: 4

Ingredients:

- 12 ounces spaghetti
- 2 tablespoons olive oil
- 4 cloves garlic, minced
- 2 tablespoons all-purpose flour (or arrowroot powder for gluten-free)
- 2 cups unsweetened almond milk
- 1/2 cup vegan parmesan cheese
- 2 tablespoons nutritional yeast
- 1/2 teaspoon salt
- 1/4 teaspoon black pepper
- Fresh parsley, chopped (for garnish, optional)

Directions:

1. To prepare the spaghetti, follow the instructions on the package and cook it until it reaches the desired al dente consistency. After cooking, drain the spaghetti and set it aside to be used later.
2. Start by warming the olive oil in a large skillet over medium heat until it reaches the desired temperature. Add minced garlic to the skillet and sauté until it becomes fragrant, which usually takes around 1-2 minutes.
3. Sprinkle the flour (or arrowroot powder) over the garlic and stir well to combine. Cook for an additional minute.
4. While whisking, slowly pour the almond milk into the skillet to achieve a smooth consistency without any lumps. Allow the mixture to simmer for roughly 5-7 minutes, stirring occasionally, until the sauce achieves the desired thickness.
5. Stir in the vegan parmesan cheese, nutritional yeast, salt, and black pepper. Keep cooking the mixture for an additional 2-3 minutes until the cheese has completely melted and the sauce turns smooth and creamy.
6. Once the spaghetti is cooked, transfer it to the skillet and toss it thoroughly to ensure that each strand is coated evenly with the sauce.
7. Continue cooking for an extra 2-3 minutes, gently stirring, until the pasta is thoroughly heated.
8. Take the skillet off the heat and, if desired, add a garnish of fresh parsley.

9. Serve the creamy vegan alfredo hot.

Nutritional breakdown per serving(1/4 of the recipe):

Calories: 400 kcal, Protein: 12 grams, Carbohydrates: 58 grams, Fat: 14 grams, Saturated Fat: 2 grams, Cholesterol: 0 milligrams, Sodium: 550 milligrams, Fiber: 4 grams, and Sugar: 2 grams.

TOMATO BASIL PASTA

Prep Time: 10 minutes
Cooking Time: 15 minutes
Total Time: 25 minutes
Servings: 4

Ingredients:

- 12 ounces spaghetti
- 2 tablespoons olive oil
- 4 cloves garlic, minced
- 2 cups cherry tomatoes, halved
- 1/4 teaspoon red pepper flakes
- Salt, to taste
- Fresh basil leaves, chopped
- Grated Parmesan cheese, for serving (optional)

Directions:

1. To prepare the spaghetti, follow the instructions on the package for cooking it until it reaches the desired al dente texture. After cooking, drain the spaghetti and set it aside for later use.
2. In a large skillet set over medium heat, warm the olive oil until it reaches the desired temperature. Once the oil is hot, sauté the minced garlic for 1-2 minutes until it becomes fragrant.
3. In the skillet, mix together the cherry tomatoes and red pepper flakes, then proceed to cook the mixture for approximately 5-7 minutes. While cooking, remember to stir the mixture occasionally until the tomatoes become tender and start to release their juices.
4. Season with salt to taste.
5. Combine the cooked spaghetti with the tomato mixture in the skillet and thoroughly toss the ingredients together to ensure that the pasta is evenly coated.
6. Let the mixture cook for an extra 2-3 minutes, gently stirring it, until the pasta is thoroughly heated and reaches the desired temperature.
7. Take the skillet off the heat and incorporate the chopped fresh basil leaves by stirring them into the mixture.
8. Serve the tomato basil pasta hot, garnished with grated Parmesan cheese if desired.

Nutritional breakdown per serving(1/4 of the recipe):

Calories: 350 kcal, Protein: 10 grams, Carbohydrates: 60 grams, Fat: 8 grams, Saturated Fat: 1 grams, Cholesterol: 0 milligrams, Sodium: 150 milligrams, Fiber: 4 grams, and Sugar: 4 grams.

LEMON GARLIC PASTA

Prep Time: 10 minutes
Cooking Time: 15 minutes
Total Time: 25 minutes
Servings: 4

Ingredients:

- 12 ounces spaghetti
- 3 tablespoons olive oil
- 4 cloves garlic, minced
- 1/4 teaspoon red pepper flakes
- Salt, to taste
- Juice and zest of 1 large lemon
- 1/4 cup chopped fresh parsley
- Grated Parmesan cheese, for serving (optional)

Directions:

1. Cook the spaghetti according to the instructions provided on the package until it reaches the desired al dente texture. After cooking, drain the spaghetti and keep it aside for future use.
2. In a large skillet over medium heat, warm the olive oil until it reaches the desired temperature. Next, add the diced onion, carrots, and celery to the skillet. Sauté the vegetables for 5-7 minutes until they begin to soften.
3. Season with salt to taste.
4. Combine the cooked spaghetti with the garlic-infused oil in the skillet and thoroughly toss to ensure that the pasta is evenly coated.
5. Pour the lemon juice over the pasta, then sprinkle the lemon zest on top. Toss the pasta once more to ensure that the flavors are evenly distributed.
6. Continue cooking the mixture for an additional 2-3 minutes, gently stirring it, until the pasta is heated through and reaches the desired temperature.
7. Take the mixture off the heat and incorporate the chopped fresh parsley by stirring it in.
8. Serve the lemon garlic pasta hot, garnished with grated Parmesan cheese if desired.

Nutritional breakdown per serving (1/4 of the recipe):

Calories: 350 kcal, Protein: 9 grams, Carbohydrates: 54 grams, Fat: 11 grams, Saturated Fat: 2 grams, Cholesterol: 0 milligrams, Sodium: 150 milligrams, Fiber: 3 grams, and Sugar: 2 grams.

VEGAN BOLOGNESE

Prep Time: 15 minutes
Cooking Time: 1 hour
Total Time: 1 hour 15 minutes
Servings: 4

Ingredients:

- 1 tablespoon olive oil
- 1 medium onion, finely diced
- 2 medium carrots, finely diced
- 2 celery stalks, finely diced
- 8 ounces mushrooms, finely chopped
- 1/2 cup walnuts, finely chopped
- 4 cloves garlic, minced
- 1 tablespoon tomato paste
- 1/4 cup red wine (optional)
- 1 can (14 ounces) crushed tomatoes
- 1 teaspoon dried oregano
- 1 teaspoon dried basil
- 1/2 teaspoon dried thyme
- Salt and pepper, to taste
- 1/4 cup fresh basil leaves, chopped
- Cooked pasta of your choice

Directions:

1. In a large skillet, heat the olive oil over medium heat until it is thoroughly warmed. Then, introduce the diced onion, carrots, and celery to the skillet. Sauté the vegetables for 5-7 minutes, or until they begin to soften.
2. Add the chopped mushrooms and walnuts to the skillet. Cook for another 5 minutes until the mushrooms release their moisture and start to brown.
3. Incorporate the minced garlic and tomato paste into the skillet, stirring them together. Cook the mixture for approximately 1 minute until it becomes fragrant.
4. If using red wine, pour it into the skillet and cook for 2-3 minutes until the alcohol evaporates.
5. Add the crushed tomatoes, dried oregano, dried basil, dried thyme, salt, and pepper. Stir well to combine.

6. Once the heat is lowered to low, let the sauce simmer for 45 minutes to allow the flavors to meld together. Stir the sauce occasionally during this time to ensure even cooking.
7. Taste and adjust the seasoning if needed.
8. Before serving, incorporate the fresh basil leaves into the dish by stirring them in.
9. Serve the vegan Bolognese sauce over cooked pasta of your choice.

Nutritional breakdown per serving(1/4 of the recipe):

Calories: 250 kcal, Protein: 7 grams, Carbohydrates: 30 grams, Fat: 12 grams, Saturated Fat: 1 grams, Cholesterol: 0 milligrams, Sodium: 350 milligrams, Fiber: 7 grams, and Sugar: 10 grams.

CREAMY MUSHROOM PASTA

Prep Time: 10 minutes
Cooking Time: 15 minutes
Total Time: 25 minutes
Servings: 4

Ingredients:

- 12 ounces of fettuccine or any pasta variety
- 1 pound mushrooms, sliced
- 2 tablespoons butter (or vegan butter for a vegan option)
- 1 tablespoon olive oil
- 2 shallots, minced
- 4 cloves garlic, minced
- 1/2 cup heavy cream or coconut cream (vegan option)
- 1 1/2 oz grated Parmesan cheese or nutritional yeast (for a vegan option)
- Salt and pepper, to taste
- Fresh parsley, chopped (for garnish, optional)

Directions:

1. Prepare the pasta by following the instructions provided on the packaging until it reaches the desired al dente texture. After cooking, drain the pasta and keep it aside for future use.
2. In a large skillet, melt the butter over medium heat and simultaneously heat the olive oil in the same skillet. Afterward, introduce the sliced mushrooms to the skillet and cook them for approximately 5-7 minutes until they release their moisture and begin to brown.
3. Incorporate the minced shallots and garlic into the skillet, ensuring they are evenly distributed. Proceed to sauté the mixture for an additional 2-3 minutes until it emits a fragrant aroma.
4. Gradually pour the heavy cream (or coconut cream) into the skillet, making sure to stir thoroughly to achieve a cohesive mixture. Allow the sauce to cook for approximately 2-3 minutes until it slightly thickens.
5. Incorporate the cooked pasta into the skillet with the creamy mushroom sauce, making sure to coat the pasta evenly. Gently mix the ingredients together, ensuring they are thoroughly combined and evenly distributed throughout the dish.
6. Continue cooking for an additional 2-3 minutes, gently stirring the mixture, until the pasta is thoroughly heated.

7. Let the mixture cook for an additional 2-3 minutes, giving it a gentle stir, to ensure that the pasta is thoroughly heated.
8. Once removed from the heat, consider garnishing the dish with fresh parsley to add a touch of freshness, if desired.
9. Serve the creamy mushroom pasta hot.

Nutritional breakdown per serving(1/4 of the recipe):

Calories: 450 kcal, Protein: 12 grams, Carbohydrates: 55 grams, Fat: 20 grams, Saturated Fat: 10 grams, Cholesterol: 0 milligrams, Sodium: 350 milligrams, Fiber: 4 grams, and Sugar: 4 grams.

PESTO PASTA

Prep Time: 10 minutes
Cooking Time: 15 minutes
Total Time: 25 minutes
Servings: 4

Ingredients:

- 12 oz fettuccine or pasta of choice
- 2 cups fresh basil leaves, packed
- 1/2 cup pine nuts, lightly toasted
- 2 cloves garlic
- 1/2 cup grated Parmesan cheese
- 1/2 cup extra-virgin olive oil
- Salt and pepper, to taste
- Fresh basil leaves, chopped (for garnish, optional)

Directions:

1. Prepare the pasta by following the instructions provided on the packaging until it reaches the desired al dente texture. After cooking, drain the pasta and keep it aside for future use.
2. In the food processor, add the fresh basil leaves, pine nuts, garlic, and grated Parmesan cheese, making sure that all the ingredients are thoroughly combined. Utilize the pulse function to finely chop the ingredients until they achieve the desired consistency.
3. While the food processor is in operation, slowly and cautiously pour the olive oil into the mixture. Maintain a controlled and steady stream as you continue adding the oil until the ingredients combine and achieve a smooth, paste-like texture.
4. Sample the pesto and add salt and pepper based on your personal preference. If required, modify the seasoning to achieve the desired taste.
5. In a large skillet set over medium heat, heat a tablespoon of olive oil until it reaches the desired temperature for cooking. Then, introduce the cooked pasta to the skillet and carefully toss it to ensure that each strand is thoroughly coated with the oil.
6. Add the desired amount of pesto to the skillet and toss well to evenly distribute the sauce.
7. Continue cooking for an extra 2-3 minutes, gently stirring the mixture, until the pasta is thoroughly heated and warmed through.
8. To enhance the dish's visual appeal, consider adding a finishing touch of fresh basil leaves as a garnish after removing it from the heat source, if desired.

9. Serve the pesto pasta hot.

Nutritional breakdown per serving(1/4 of the recipe):

Calories: 600 kcal, Protein: 12 grams, Carbohydrates: 38 grams, Fat: 47 grams, Saturated Fat: 7 grams, Cholesterol: 0 milligrams, Sodium: 250 milligrams, Fiber: 3 grams, and Sugar: 2 grams.

ROASTED VEGETABLE PASTA

Prep Time: 15 minutes
Cooking Time: 30 minutes
Total Time: 45 minutes
Servings: 4

Ingredients:

- 12 ounces penne pasta
- 1 green bell pepper, sliced
- 1 red onion, sliced
- 1 zucchini, sliced
- 8 ounces mushrooms, sliced
- 2 carrots, sliced
- 1 cup cherry tomatoes
- 3 cloves garlic, minced
- 2 tablespoons olive oil
- Salt and pepper, to taste
- Fresh parsley, chopped
- Grated Parmesan cheese, for serving

Directions:

1. Start the cooking preparations by preheating the oven to 425°F (220°C), ensuring that it reaches the desired temperature required for the recipe.
2. In a large baking sheet, spread out the sliced bell pepper, red onion, zucchini, mushrooms, carrots, and cherry tomatoes.
3. Coat the vegetables by drizzling them with olive oil and evenly sprinkling minced garlic, salt, and pepper. Toss the ingredients thoroughly to ensure they are well coated.
4. Transfer the vegetables to the preheated oven and allow them to roast for around 20-25 minutes, or until they become tender and develop a delightful caramelized texture.
5. While the vegetables are in the process of roasting, diligently adhere to the instructions provided on the pasta package to cook it until it reaches the desired level of doneness, commonly known as "al dente." After cooking the pasta, ensure that it is thoroughly drained and set it aside, reserving it for later inclusion in the recipe.
6. Next, introduce the roasted vegetables and cooked pasta to the skillet, ensuring they are evenly distributed. Toss the ingredients together diligently to achieve a thorough combination.

7. Continue cooking the mixture for an additional 2-3 minutes, while stirring gently, until the pasta is thoroughly heated. This step ensures that every part of the pasta is evenly warmed and ready to be served.
8. If desired, remove the dish from the heat source and consider adding a fresh parsley garnish.
9. Serve the roasted vegetable pasta hot, with grated Parmesan cheese (or nutritional yeast) on top.

Nutritional breakdown per serving(1/4 of the recipe):

Calories: 350 kcal, Protein: 12 grams, Carbohydrates: 55 grams, Fat: 10 grams, Saturated Fat: 2 grams, Cholesterol: 0 milligrams, Sodium: 150 milligrams, Fiber: 7 grams, and Sugar: 9 grams.

VEGAN CARBONARA

Prep Time: 15 minutes
Cooking Time: 15 minutes
Total Time: 30 minutes
Servings: 4

Ingredients:

For the Egg Sauce:

- 1/2 cup raw cashews (100g)
- 1/2 cup nutritional yeast (15g)
- 1 teaspoon turmeric
- 1 tablespoon Dijon mustard
- 1/2 teaspoon garlic powder
- 1/2 teaspoon onion powder
- 1/2 teaspoon black salt
- 1 cup of soy milk (240ml) or any non-dairy milk

For the Pasta:

- 8 oz spaghetti (226g) dry

For the Mushrooms:

- 1 tablespoon vegan butter
- 2 cups mushrooms (240g) sliced
- 2 teaspoons crushed garlic
- 1/2 teaspoon smoked paprika
- 1/2 teaspoon sea salt
- 1/2 teaspoon black pepper

For Serving:

- Fresh chopped parsley

Instructions:

1. Once you have gathered the ingredients for the egg sauce, place them in a blender and blend until a smooth and uniform consistency is obtained. After blending, set the sauce aside, reserving it for future use in the recipe.
2. To achieve the desired level of doneness, commonly referred to as "al dente," carefully follow the cooking instructions provided on the spaghetti package. After cooking, ensure that the spaghetti is thoroughly drained and then set it aside, reserving it for future use in the recipe.
3. Heat a large skillet over medium heat and melt the vegan butter until completely liquefied. Proceed by adding the sliced mushrooms to the skillet and cook them for approximately 5-7 minutes. Keep an eye on them until they start releasing their moisture and attain a desirable golden-brown hue.
4. Add the crushed garlic, smoked paprika, sea salt, and black pepper to the skillet. Cook for another 2-3 minutes until fragrant.
5. Pour the egg sauce into the skillet and stir well to combine with the mushrooms. Continue cooking the sauce for a duration of 2-3 minutes, allowing it to thicken slightly.
6. Introduce the cooked spaghetti to the skillet and toss it thoroughly to ensure that the pasta is evenly coated with the creamy mushroom sauce.
7. Continue cooking the mixture for an additional 2-3 minutes, ensuring to give it a gentle stir, until the pasta is evenly heated throughout.
8. When the skillet is no longer on the heat source, utilize this opportunity to enhance the dish by sprinkling a final flourish of freshly chopped parsley as a garnish.
9. Serve the vegan carbonara hot.

Nutritional breakdown per serving(1/4 of the recipe):

Calories: 400 kcal, Protein: 15 grams, Carbohydrates: 60 grams, Fat: 12 grams, Saturated Fat: 2 grams, Cholesterol: 0 milligrams, Sodium: 500 milligrams, Fiber: 7 grams, and Sugar: 3 grams.

CHAPTER 5:
MEAT, POULTRY
AND SAFOOD
RECIPES

GRILLED STEAK

Prep Time: 10 minutes
Cooking Time: 10 minutes
Total Time: 20 minutes
Servings: 4

Ingredients:

- 4 steaks (such as ribeye, sirloin, or filet mignon), about 8 ounces each
- 2 tablespoons olive oil
- 2 cloves garlic, minced
- 1 teaspoon dried thyme
- 1 teaspoon dried rosemary
- Salt and pepper, to taste

Directions:

1. Preheat the grill to medium-high heat.
2. In a small bowl, combine the olive oil, minced garlic, dried thyme, dried rosemary, salt, and pepper. Mix well to create a marinade.
3. After using a paper towel to gently dry the steaks, apply the marinade by brushing both sides of the steaks.
4. Position the steaks onto the preheated grill and proceed to cook them for approximately 4-5 minutes per side to attain a medium-rare doneness. Alternatively, you can modify the cooking time to suit your preferred level of doneness.
5. When the steaks have achieved your desired level of doneness, handle them with care as you remove them from the grill. It is important to let them rest for a few minutes before serving.
6. Serve the grilled steaks hot with your choice of side dishes.

Nutritional breakdown per serving (1 steak):

Calories: 400 kcal, Protein: 30 grams, Carbohydrates: 0 grams, Fat: 30 grams, Saturated Fat: 10 grams, Cholesterol: 100 milligrams, Sodium: 108 milligrams, Fiber: 0 grams, and Sugar: 0 grams.

BAKED LEMON HERB CHICKEN

Prep Time: 15 minutes
Cooking Time: 30 minutes
Total Time: 45 minutes
Servings: 4

Ingredients:

- 4 boneless, skinless chicken breasts
- 1/4 cup olive oil
- 1/4 cup freshly squeezed lemon juice
- 3 cloves garlic, minced
- 1 teaspoon salt
- 1/2 teaspoon dried thyme
- 1/2 teaspoon dried oregano
- 1/4 teaspoon black pepper
- 1 large lemon, thinly sliced
- 1 teaspoon paprika
- 1/2 teaspoon garlic powder
- Fresh parsley, chopped (for garnish, optional)

Directions:

1. Start the cooking preparations by preheating the oven to 425°F (220°C), ensuring that it reaches the desired temperature required for the recipe.
2. In a small bowl, whisk together the olive oil, lemon juice, minced garlic, salt, dried thyme, dried oregano, and black pepper.
3. Position the chicken breasts in a baking dish, making sure they are evenly distributed across the surface of the dish. Proceed to pour the lemon herb marinade over the chicken breasts, making certain to coat each piece thoroughly.
4. Arrange the lemon slices on top of the chicken breasts.
5. In a separate small bowl, mix together the paprika and garlic powder. Evenly distribute this mixture by sprinkling it over the chicken breasts.
6. For the chicken to be thoroughly cooked, it is important to follow these steps: Place the chicken in a preheated oven and bake it for approximately 25-30 minutes, ensuring that the internal temperature reaches 165°F (74°C).
7. Before serving, it is important to let the chicken rest for a few minutes once it has been taken out of the oven.
8. Garnish with fresh chopped parsley, if desired.

9. Serve the baked lemon herb chicken hot, with your choice of side dishes.

Nutritional breakdown per serving (1 chicken breast):

Calories: 300 kcal, Protein: 35 grams, Carbohydrates: 5 grams, Fat: 15 grams, Saturated Fat: 2 grams, Cholesterol: 85 milligrams, Sodium: 500 milligrams, Fiber: 1 grams, and Sugar: 1 grams.

SHRIMP SCAMPI

Prep Time: 15 minutes
Cooking Time: 30 minutes
Total Time: 45 minutes
Servings: 4

Ingredients:

- 4 boneless, skinless chicken breasts
- 1/4 cup olive oil
- 1/4 cup freshly squeezed lemon juice
- 3 cloves garlic, minced
- 1 teaspoon salt
- 1/2 teaspoon dried thyme
- 1/2 teaspoon dried rosemary
- 1/4 teaspoon black pepper
- 1 large lemon, thinly sliced
- 1 teaspoon paprika
- 1/2 teaspoon garlic powder
- Fresh parsley, chopped (for garnish, optional)

Directions:

1. Start the cooking preparations by preheating the oven to 425°F (220°C), ensuring that it reaches the desired temperature required for the recipe.
2. In a small bowl, whisk together the olive oil, lemon juice, minced garlic, salt, dried thyme, dried rosemary, and black pepper.
3. Arrange the salmon fillets in an even and spaced-out manner on a baking sheet lined with either parchment paper or aluminum foil.
4. Brush the honey mustard glaze evenly over the salmon fillets, coating the tops and sides.
5. In a separate small bowl, mix together the paprika and garlic powder. Ensure an even distribution of the mixture by sprinkling it over the chicken breasts.
6. Once the salmon is positioned in the preheated oven, allow it to bake for around 12-15 minutes, or until it acquires an opaque color and can be effortlessly flaked using a fork.
7. After removing the salmon from the oven, it is recommended to let it rest for a few minutes before serving.
8. To add an optional final touch, consider garnishing with freshly chopped parsley.

9. Serve the baked lemon herb chicken hot, with your choice of side dishes.

Nutritional breakdown per serving(1 chicken breast):

Calories: 300 kcal, Protein: 52 grams, Carbohydrates: 4 grams, Fat: 15 grams, Saturated Fat: 2 grams, Cholesterol: 200 milligrams, Sodium: 2322 milligrams, Fiber: 0 grams, and Sugar: 0 grams.

HONEY MUSTARD GLAZED SALMON

Prep Time: 10 minutes
Cooking Time: 15 minutes
Total Time: 25 minutes
Servings: 4

Ingredients:

- 4 salmon fillets, about 6 ounces each
- 2 tablespoons Dijon mustard
- 2 tablespoons honey
- 2 cloves garlic, minced
- 1 tablespoon olive oil
- Salt and pepper, to taste
- Fresh parsley, chopped (for garnish, optional)

Directions:

1. Start the cooking preparations by preheating the oven to 400°F (200°C), ensuring that it reaches the desired temperature required for the recipe.
2. In a small bowl, whisk together the Dijon mustard, honey, minced garlic, olive oil, salt, and pepper.
3. Delicately place the salmon fillets onto a prepared baking sheet, which can be lined with either parchment paper or aluminum foil. Ensure that they are positioned in a tidy and well-organized manner.
4. Brush the honey mustard glaze evenly over the salmon fillets, coating the tops and sides.
5. Insert the salmon into the preheated oven and let it cook for 12-15 minutes, or until it reaches an opaque state and can be effortlessly flaked with a fork.
6. Retrieve the salmon from the oven and grant it a brief period of rest for a few minutes prior to serving.
7. Garnish with fresh chopped parsley, if desired.
8. Serve the honey mustard glazed salmon hot, with your choice of side dishes.

Nutritional breakdown per serving (1 salmon fillet):

Calories: 350 kcal, Protein: 34 grams, Carbohydrates: 10 grams, Fat: 18 grams, Saturated Fat: 3 grams, Cholesterol: 50 milligrams, Sodium: 350 milligrams, Fiber: 0 grams, and Sugar: 9 grams.

CHICKEN FAJITAS

Prep Time: 15 minutes
Cooking Time: 15 minutes
Total Time: 30 minutes
Servings: 4

Ingredients:

For the Fajita Seasoning:

- 1/2 tablespoon chili powder
- 1/2 tablespoon ground cumin
- 1 teaspoon garlic powder
- 1/2 teaspoon paprika
- 1/2 teaspoon dried oregano
- 1/2 teaspoon salt
- 1/4 teaspoon black pepper

For the Chicken Fajitas:

- 1 lb (450g) chicken breasts, boneless and skinless, sliced
- 2 tablespoons cooking oil
- 1 large onion, thinly sliced
- 3 bell peppers (any color), thinly sliced
- 8 small flour tortillas
- Optional toppings: sour cream, guacamole, pico de gallo, shredded cheese, lime wedges, fresh cilantro

Directions:

1. To prepare the fajita seasoning, combine all the ingredients in a small bowl and mix well.
2. Evenly distribute the fajita seasoning on both sides of the sliced chicken breasts, ensuring that it adheres to the chicken by pressing it gently.
3. Commence by heating the cooking oil in a large skillet or pan over medium-high heat until it reaches the desired temperature.
4. Once the skillet is heated, add the seasoned chicken and cook it for approximately 5-6 minutes until it is thoroughly cooked and has a golden brown color. Afterwards, remove the chicken from the skillet and set it aside for later use.

5. Subsequently, introduce the sliced onion and bell peppers into the identical skillet. Proceed to cook the vegetables for an estimated 5 minutes, or until they achieve a tender-crisp consistency.
6. After combining the cooked chicken and vegetables in the skillet, ensure they are mixed thoroughly. Continue cooking the mixture for an extra 1-2 minutes, ensuring that all the components are evenly heated.
7. To warm the flour tortillas, carefully follow the instructions provided on the package.
8. After warming the tortillas, transfer the chicken fajita mixture onto them. Enhance the dish by adding your favorite toppings, including sour cream, guacamole, pico de gallo, shredded cheese, lime wedges, and fresh cilantro.
9. Fold the tortillas and enjoy the delicious chicken fajitas.

Nutritional breakdown per serving(1 serving with tortilla, without toppings):

Calories: 350 kcal, Protein: 30 grams, Carbohydrates: 35 grams, Fat: 10 grams, Saturated Fat: 2 grams, Cholesterol: 100 milligrams, Sodium: 700 milligrams, Fiber: 4 grams, and Sugar: 5 grams.

PAN-SEARED PORK CHOPS

Prep Time: 5 minutes
Cooking Time: 10 minutes
Total Time: 15 minutes
Servings: 4

Ingredients:

- 4 bone-in pork chops, approximately 1 inch thick
- 1 tablespoon olive oil
- 1 teaspoon salt
- 1/2 teaspoon black pepper
- 1/2 teaspoon garlic powder
- 1/2 teaspoon paprika
- Optional: fresh herbs for garnish (such as thyme or rosemary)

Directions:

1. To create a flavorful blend, combine the salt, black pepper, garlic powder, and paprika in a small bowl, ensuring all ingredients are thoroughly mixed.
2. Ensure the pork chops are thoroughly dried by gently patting them with a paper towel. Then, generously season each side of the chops with the spice mixture, making sure to cover them evenly.
3. Start the cooking process by heating the olive oil in a large skillet over medium-high heat until it reaches the desired temperature.
4. After the oil has reached the desired temperature, proceed by placing the pork chops into the skillet. Let them cook for about 4-5 minutes on each side, or until the internal temperature reaches 145°F (63°C) for a medium-rare doneness level, or 160°F (71°C) for a medium doneness level. Make sure to use a meat thermometer to accurately gauge the temperature.
5. Remove the pork chops from the skillet and let them rest for a few minutes before serving.
6. Optional: Garnish with fresh herbs, such as thyme or rosemary, before serving.
7. Serve the pan-seared pork chops hot, with your choice of side dishes.

Nutritional breakdown per serving(1 pork chop):

Calories: 250 kcal, Protein: 27 grams, Carbohydrates: 0 grams, Fat: 15 grams, Saturated Fat: 4 grams, Cholesterol: 80 milligrams, Sodium: 500 milligrams, Fiber: 0 grams, and Sugar: 0 grams.

LEMON GARLIC SHRIMP PASTA

Prep Time: 10 minutes
Cooking Time: 15 minutes
Total Time: 25 minutes
Servings: 4

Ingredients:

- 8 ounces pasta (linguine, spaghetti, or your favorite long pasta)
- 2 tablespoons olive oil
- 2 tablespoons butter
- 2 tablespoons minced garlic
- 1/4 teaspoon crushed red pepper flakes
- 1 pound shrimp, peeled and deveined
- Zest and juice of 1 large lemon
- 1/4 cup chopped fresh parsley
- Salt and pepper, to taste
- Optional: Grated Parmesan cheese for serving

Directions:

1. To start cooking the pasta, take a look at the instructions provided on the pasta package. Follow the instructions diligently to cook the pasta in salted water until it reaches the desired al dente texture. After the pasta is cooked, carefully drain the water and set the pasta aside for later use.
2. Place a large skillet over medium heat and gently warm the olive oil and butter until they reach the desired temperature.
3. Once the skillet is ready, incorporate the minced garlic and, if desired, crushed red pepper flakes. Sauté the mixture for around one minute until it becomes fragrant.
4. Place the shrimp in the skillet and cook for about 2-3 minutes on each side until they turn pink and are fully cooked.
5. Combine the lemon zest, lemon juice, and chopped parsley into the mixture, stirring until well incorporated. Customize the flavor by adding salt and pepper to suit your personal taste.
6. Introduce the cooked pasta into the skillet and mix it thoroughly to ensure that the pasta is evenly coated with the lemon garlic sauce.
7. To serve, present the lemon garlic shrimp pasta while hot, optionally garnished with additional chopped parsley and grated Parmesan cheese for added flavor.

Nutritional breakdown per serving(1 serving without Parmesan cheese):

Calories: 400 kcal, Protein: 24 grams, Carbohydrates: 46 grams, Fat: 14 grams, Saturated Fat: 5 grams, Cholesterol: 250 milligrams, Sodium: 400 milligrams, Fiber: 2 grams, and Sugar: 2 grams.

TERIYAKI GLAZED CHICKEN SKEWERS

Prep Time: 15 minutes
Cooking Time: 10 minutes
Total Time: 25 minutes
Servings: 4

Ingredients:

- 1.5 lbs (680g) boneless, skinless chicken breasts, cut into 1-inch cubes
- 1/4 cup soy sauce
- 2 tablespoons honey
- 2 tablespoons rice vinegar
- 2 cloves garlic, minced
- 1 teaspoon grated fresh ginger
- 1 tablespoon cornstarch
- 1 tablespoon water
- To add a finishing touch, you may choose to include sesame seeds and finely chopped green onions as a garnish
- Submerge the bamboo skewers in water for a duration of 30 minutes

Directions:

1. Mix the soy sauce, honey, rice vinegar, minced garlic, and grated ginger in a small bowl to make the teriyaki sauce. Use a whisk to blend the ingredients until the sauce becomes smooth and flavorful.
2. To prepare a slurry, combine cornstarch and water in a separate small bowl. Mix the two ingredients together until they form a smooth mixture.
3. In a large bowl, pour half of the teriyaki sauce over the chicken cubes and toss to coat. Let it marinate for 10 minutes.
4. To ensure the grill or grill pan is ready for cooking, preheat it over medium-high heat before grilling.
5. Take the marinated chicken and carefully thread it onto the bamboo skewers that have been soaked.
6. Grill the chicken skewers for about 4-5 minutes on each side, or until the chicken is cooked through and has a nice char.
7. As the chicken grills, take a small saucepan and heat the remaining teriyaki sauce over medium heat. Continuously stir the cornstarch slurry into the saucepan until the sauce reaches the desired thickness.
8. Take the chicken skewers off the grill and apply a generous coating of the thickened teriyaki sauce.

9. If desired, you can add a garnish of sesame seeds and chopped green onions to enhance the presentation.
10. Serve the teriyaki glazed chicken skewers hot, with steamed rice and your favorite vegetables.

Nutritional breakdown per serving(1 serving, without rice and garnishes):

Calories: 250 kcal, Protein: 35 grams, Carbohydrates: 18 grams, Fat: 3 grams, Saturated Fat: 1 grams, Cholesterol: 100 milligrams, Sodium: 800 milligrams, Fiber: 0 grams, and Sugar: 14 grams.

SEARED SCALLOPS

Prep Time: 5 minutes
Cooking Time: 5 minutes
Total Time: 10 minutes
Servings: 2-4

Ingredients:

- 1 lb dry sea scallops
- Salt and pepper, to taste
- 1 tablespoon vegetable oil
- 2 tablespoons butter
- Optional: Fresh thyme, garlic, or other aromatics
- Lemon wedges, for serving

Directions:

1. After rinsing the scallops, gently pat them dry using paper towels. Season them with salt, pepper, and any additional aromatics you prefer, such as fresh thyme or garlic powder.
2. To begin the cooking process, make sure to heat the large skillet over medium-high heat until it reaches the desired temperature. Next, carefully add the vegetable oil to the skillet.
3. Place the scallops in the skillet in a single layer, ensuring they are not touching one another. Allow the scallops to sear for approximately 3 minutes on each side, or until a desirable golden brown crust forms.
4. Next, add the butter to the skillet and allow it to melt. Swirl the melted butter around the scallops, ensuring they are coated evenly. Baste the scallops with the melted butter to enhance and enrich their flavor.
5. Carefully remove the scallops from the skillet and gently transfer them to a plate. Squeeze fresh lemon juice over the scallops.
6. Serve the seared scallops immediately, garnished with lemon wedges.

Nutritional breakdown per serving(1 serving, without optional aromatics):

Calories: 185 kcal, Protein: 23 grams, Carbohydrates: 6 grams, Fat: 8 grams, Saturated Fat: 1 grams, Cholesterol: 40 milligrams, Sodium: 400 milligrams, Fiber: 0 grams, and Sugar: 0 grams.

BEEF STIR-FRY

Prep Time: 15 minutes
Cooking Time: 10 minutes
Total Time: 25 minutes
Servings: 4

Ingredients:

- 1 lb (450g) beef sirloin, thinly sliced against the grain
- Salt and pepper, to taste
- 2 tablespoons vegetable oil
- 2 cloves garlic, minced
- 1 tablespoon grated fresh ginger
- 1 red bell pepper, thinly sliced
- 1 yellow bell pepper, thinly sliced
- 1 small onion, thinly sliced
- 2 cups broccoli florets
- 1/4 cup low-sodium soy sauce
- 2 tablespoons oyster sauce
- 1 tablespoon honey
- If desired, add sesame seeds and sliced green onions as a garnish
- Cooked rice or noodles, for serving

Directions:

1. To enhance the flavor of the thinly sliced beef, sprinkle it with some salt and pepper.
2. To commence, heat a large skillet or wok over high heat until it becomes hot. Subsequently, add 1 tablespoon of vegetable oil to the skillet or wok.
3. Place the beef in the skillet and stir-fry it for 2-3 minutes until it is nicely browned. Once done, remove the beef from the skillet and set it aside.
4. Afterward, add the remaining tablespoon of vegetable oil to the skillet.
5. Incorporate the minced garlic and grated ginger into the skillet, and stir-fry the mixture for around 30 seconds until a delightful fragrance permeates the air.
6. Include the sliced bell peppers, onion, and broccoli florets in the skillet. Proceed to stir-fry the assortment for a duration of 3-4 minutes, or until the vegetables reach a desired level of tenderness while still maintaining a slight crunch.
7. Combine the soy sauce, oyster sauce, and honey in a small bowl and whisk them together until well blended.

8. Reintroduce the cooked beef to the skillet and generously pour the sauce over the beef and vegetables. Proceed to stir-fry the mixture for an additional 1-2 minutes, ensuring that everything is evenly coated and heated through.
9. Take the skillet off the heat and, if desired, enhance the presentation by sprinkling sesame seeds and sliced green onions as a garnish.
10. Serve the beef stir-fry hot over cooked rice or noodles.

Nutritional breakdown per serving(1 serving without rice/noodles and garnishes):

Calories: 280 kcal, Protein: 26 grams, Carbohydrates: 14 grams, Fat: 14 grams, Saturated Fat: 4 grams, Cholesterol: 80 milligrams, Sodium: 800 milligrams, Fiber: 3 grams, and Sugar: 8 grams.

GRILLED HONEY LIME CHICKEN

Prep Time: 10 minutes

Cooking Time: 15 minutes

Total Time: 25 minutes

Servings: 4

Ingredients:

- 1.5 lbs (680g) boneless, skinless chicken breasts
- Juice and zest of 2 limes
- 3 tablespoons honey
- 2 tablespoons soy sauce
- 2 cloves garlic, minced
- 1 tablespoon vegetable oil
- Salt and pepper, to taste
- Optional: Chopped fresh cilantro for garnish

Directions:

1. In a small bowl, whisk together the lime juice, lime zest, honey, soy sauce, minced garlic, vegetable oil, salt, and pepper to make the marinade.
2. Position the chicken breasts in either a shallow dish or a resealable plastic bag. Thoroughly coat the chicken with the marinade, ensuring an even distribution.
3. To enhance the flavor, let the chicken marinate in the refrigerator for at least 30 minutes. For a more intensified taste, refrigerate it for up to 4 hours.
4. Prior to grilling, ensure that the grill is preheated to a medium-high heat.
5. Once the marinating process is complete, carefully take out the chicken from the marinade, ensuring that any surplus marinade is allowed to drip off.
6. To ensure optimal results when grilling, it is recommended to cook each side of the chicken for approximately 6-8 minutes or until the internal temperature reaches 165°F (74°C). It is recommended to use a meat thermometer to ensure accurate measurement.
7. After the grilling process is finished, gently take the chicken off the grill and set it aside to rest for a few minutes. This resting period is important before proceeding to slice the chicken.
8. Slice the grilled chicken and garnish with chopped fresh cilantro, if desired.
9. Serve the grilled honey lime chicken hot, with your choice of side dishes.

Nutritional breakdown per serving:

Calories: 250 kcal, Protein: 35 grams, Carbohydrates: 17 grams, Fat: 5 grams, Saturated Fat: 1 grams, Cholesterol: 100 milligrams, Sodium: 350 milligrams, Fiber: 0 grams, and Sugar: 15 grams.

BAKED COD WITH ROASTED VEGETABLES

Prep Time: 15 minutes
Cooking Time: 40 minutes
Total Time: 55 minutes
Servings: 4

Ingredients:

- 2 lbs (900g) cod fillets
- 5 small carrots, diced
- 1 large onion, diced
- 2 cups chopped celery
- 1 large bell pepper, diced
- 16 oz roasted garlic pasta sauce
- 1 tablespoon salt, adjust to taste
- 1/2 tablespoon ground black pepper, adjust to taste
- 2 tablespoons oil (avocado or olive)

Directions:

1. Start the cooking preparations by preheating the oven to 350°F (175°C), ensuring that it reaches the desired temperature required for the recipe.
2. In a large skillet, sauté the diced carrots, onion, celery, and bell pepper with oil until slightly softened.
3. To combine the roasted garlic pasta sauce with the vegetables, add it to the skillet and thoroughly stir everything together.
4. To start, place the cod fillets in a baking dish, making sure to season the tops generously with salt and pepper.
5. Pour the vegetable sauce over the cod fillets, covering them completely.
6. Once you have covered the baking dish with a lid or foil, transfer it to the preheated oven. Allow it to bake for around 40 minutes, or until the cod is thoroughly cooked and can be effortlessly flaked using a fork.
7. Serve the baked cod with roasted vegetables hot, alongside your choice of side dishes.

Nutritional breakdown per serving:

Calories: 300 kcal, Protein: 32 grams, Carbohydrates: 25 grams, Fat: 8 grams, Saturated Fat: 1 grams, Cholesterol: 80 milligrams, Sodium: 500 milligrams, Fiber: 6 grams, and Sugar: 12 grams.

TURKEY MEATBALLS

Prep Time: 15 minutes
Cooking Time: 25 minutes
Total Time: 40 minutes
Servings: 4

Ingredients:

- 1 lb (450g) ground turkey
- 1/2 cup grated Parmesan cheese
- 1/2 cup panko breadcrumbs
- 1/4 cup minced onion
- 2 cloves garlic, minced
- 1/4 cup chopped fresh parsley
- 1 large egg, beaten
- 1 teaspoon dried oregano
- 1/2 teaspoon salt
- 1/4 teaspoon black pepper
- 2 tablespoons olive oil

Directions:

1. Start the cooking preparations by preheating the oven to 400°F (200°C), ensuring that it reaches the desired temperature required for the recipe.
2. In a large bowl, combine the ground turkey, grated Parmesan cheese, panko breadcrumbs, minced onion, minced garlic, chopped parsley, beaten egg, dried oregano, salt, and black pepper. Ensure that all the ingredients are mixed well until they are evenly incorporated.
3. Take the mixture and form it into meatballs, each measuring approximately 1.5 inches in diameter.
4. To commence the cooking process, you should heat the olive oil in a large skillet over medium heat. Next, carefully place the meatballs into the skillet and cook them for about 5 minutes, ensuring that they are browned on all sides.
5. Place the browned meatballs onto a baking sheet that has been lined with parchment paper, ensuring to handle them with care.
6. Bake the meatballs in the preheated oven for 15-20 minutes, or until cooked through and no longer pink in the center.
7. After the meatballs have finished cooking, carefully remove them from the oven and give them a few minutes to rest before they are ready to be served.
8. Serve the turkey meatballs with your favorite sauce, pasta, or as desired.

Nutritional breakdown per serving(1 serving, approximately 4 meatballs):

Calories: 280 kcal, Protein: 27 grams, Carbohydrates: 7 grams, Fat: 16 grams, Saturated Fat: 5 grams, Cholesterol: 80 milligrams, Sodium: 610 milligrams, Fiber: 1 grams, and Sugar: 1 grams.

COCONUT CURRY SHRIMP

Prep Time: 10 minutes
Cooking Time: 20 minutes
Total Time: 30 minutes
Servings: 4

Ingredients:

- 1 lb (450g) of peeled, deveined large shrimp
- 1 teaspoon salt
- 1/2 teaspoon black pepper
- 1/2 teaspoon cayenne pepper (adjust to taste)
- 2 tablespoons lemon juice
- 1 tablespoon coconut oil
- 1 medium onion, chopped
- 3 cloves garlic, minced
- 1 tablespoon fresh ginger, minced
- 1/2 teaspoon ground turmeric
- 1 teaspoon ground coriander
- 1 teaspoon curry powder
- 14 oz (400g) diced tomatoes
- 13 oz (370ml) coconut milk
- 2 tablespoons of chopped cilantro (or parsley) for garnishing
- Cooked rice for serving

Directions:

1. To prepare the marinade, combine the shrimp, salt, black pepper, cayenne pepper, and lemon juice in a bowl. Mix thoroughly to ensure the shrimp is evenly coated. After combining the shrimp with the marinade, set it aside and let it sit for 10 minutes before proceeding to the next step.
2. Start the cooking process by heating the coconut oil in a large skillet over medium heat. Proceed by adding the chopped onion to the skillet and sauté it until it reaches a translucent state.
3. Add the minced garlic, minced ginger, ground turmeric, ground coriander, and curry powder to the skillet. Continuously stir and cook for approximately 1 minute until the aroma is released.

4. Incorporate the diced tomatoes into the skillet, letting them simmer for around 2 to 3 minutes. This will result in a harmonious amalgamation of flavors that is sure to please the palate.
5. Gently pour the coconut milk into the mixture and stir thoroughly to ensure even distribution. Heat the combination until it reaches a gentle simmer.
6. Introduce the marinated shrimp to the skillet and allow them to cook for a duration of 5 to 7 minutes, or until they turn a vibrant pink color and are thoroughly cooked.
7. Take the skillet off the heat and embellish the dish with a sprinkle of finely chopped cilantro.
8. Serve the coconut curry shrimp hot over cooked rice.

Nutritional breakdown per serving(1 serving without rice):

Calories: 250 kcal, Protein: 20 grams, Carbohydrates: 10 grams, Fat: 15 grams, Saturated Fat: 11 grams, Cholesterol: 250 milligrams, Sodium: 800 milligrams, Fiber: 2 grams, and Sugar: 5 grams.

LEMON HERB ROASTED CHICKEN

Prep Time: 10 minutes
Cooking Time: 1 hour 30 minutes
Total Time: 1 hour 40 minutes
Servings: 4

Ingredients:

- 1 whole chicken (about 4 lbs or 1.8 kg)
- 2 lemons, divided
- 4 cloves garlic, minced
- 2 tablespoons fresh rosemary leaves, chopped
- 2 tablespoons fresh thyme leaves, chopped
- 2 tablespoons fresh parsley, chopped
- 2 tablespoons olive oil
- 1 teaspoon salt
- 1/2 teaspoon black pepper

Directions:

1. Start the cooking preparations by preheating the oven to 425°F (220°C), ensuring that it reaches the desired temperature required for the recipe.
2. Thoroughly wash the chicken both internally and externally, followed by gently drying it with paper towels.
3. Take a lemon and carefully cut it into thin slices. Set the lemon slices aside to be used at a later time.
4. Combine minced garlic, chopped rosemary, thyme, parsley, olive oil, salt, and black pepper in a small bowl, blending them until they form a delicious and fragrant herb mixture.
5. To preserve the integrity of the chicken skin, handle it with care as you gently slide your fingers between the skin and the meat, ensuring a seamless separation without causing any damage or tearing.
6. Rub the herb mixture under the skin of the chicken, spreading it evenly over the breast and thigh meat.
7. Insert the lemon slices into the cavity of the chicken, ensuring they are evenly distributed.
8. Extract the juice from the remaining lemon and drizzle it generously over the chicken, ensuring that it is evenly coated.
9. Secure the chicken's legs together using kitchen twine and neatly tuck the wings underneath the body, ensuring a compact and tidy presentation.

10. Set the chicken on a roasting pan's rack, ensuring that the breast side is facing upwards.
11. Let the chicken cook undisturbed in the preheated oven for approximately 1 hour and 30 minutes, or until the internal temperature reaches 165°F (74°C). To obtain an accurate measurement, carefully insert a meat thermometer into the thickest area of the chicken thigh, being careful not to make contact with the bone.
12. If the chicken starts to brown too quickly, cover it loosely with foil.
13. After taking the chicken out of the oven, allow it to rest undisturbed for approximately 10 minutes before you begin carving. This resting period is essential as it allows the juices to evenly distribute, resulting in a chicken that is both tastier and more tender.
14. Serve the lemon herb roasted chicken hot, with your choice of side dishes.

Nutritional breakdown per serving:

Calories: 400 kcal, Protein: 38 grams, Carbohydrates: 5 grams, Fat: 25 grams, Saturated Fat: 6 grams, Cholesterol: 100 milligrams, Sodium: 650 milligrams, Fiber: 2 grams, and Sugar: 1 grams.

CHAPTER 6
SNACKS

CAPRESE SKEWERS

Prep Time: 15 minutes
Total Time: 15 minutes
Servings: 4 (9 skewers)

Ingredients:

- 36 cherry tomatoes
- 24 mini mozzarella balls
- 36 fresh basil leaves
- 1 tablespoon extra-virgin olive oil
- 1 teaspoon Italian seasoning
- 1 tablespoon balsamic glaze
- Salt and pepper, to taste

Directions:

1. Prepare the skewers by threading one cherry tomato, one mini mozzarella ball, and one basil leaf onto each skewer. Repeat until all skewers have been assembled.
2. In a small bowl, mix together the olive oil, Italian seasoning, salt, and pepper. To create a well-blended mixture, use a whisk to thoroughly combine the ingredients until they are fully incorporated.
3. Ensure that all the components are evenly mixed together. Ensure that all components are thoroughly integrated for optimal taste.
4. Drizzle the olive oil mixture over the assembled skewers.
5. Drizzle the balsamic glaze over the skewers.
6. Serve the caprese skewers immediately as an appetizer or a light snack.

Nutritional breakdown per serving(1 serving, approximately 9 skewers):

Calories: 150 kcal, Protein: 9 grams, Carbohydrates: 6 grams, Fat: 10 grams, Saturated Fat: 4 grams, Cholesterol: 20 milligrams, Sodium: 200 milligrams, Fiber: 9 grams, and Sugar: 3 grams.

MINI QUESADILLAS

Prep Time: 10 minutes
Cooking Time: 10 minutes
Total Time: 20 minutes
Servings: 4 (approximately 16 mini quesadillas)

Ingredients:

- 8 small flour tortillas
- 1 cup shredded cheese (cheddar, Monterey Jack, or a blend)
- Optional fillings: diced cooked chicken, sautéed vegetables, black beans, corn, etc.
- Optional garnishes: sour cream, salsa, guacamole, cilantro, etc.

Directions:

1. To prepare for cooking, make sure to preheat the skillet or griddle over medium heat. This step is essential for achieving optimal cooking results.
2. Place a tortilla onto the skillet and evenly spread shredded cheese on a single side of the tortilla.
3. Should you desire, you have the option to add extra fillings on the layer of cheese.
4. Gently press down with a spatula to fold the tortilla in half, ensuring that the edges are sealed.
5. Cook each side of the tortilla for around 2-3 minutes, or until it achieves a golden brown color and the cheese has fully melted.
6. Take out the quesadilla from the skillet and proceed to repeat the same process with the remaining tortillas and fillings.
7. Cut each cooked quesadilla into quarters to create mini quesadillas.
8. Serve the mini quesadillas warm with your choice of garnishes.

Nutritional breakdown per serving(4 servings, approximately 4 mini quesadillas):

Calories: 300 kcal, Protein: 12 grams, Carbohydrates: 35 grams, Fat: 12 grams, Saturated Fat: 6 grams, Cholesterol: 30 milligrams, Sodium: 450 milligrams, Fiber: 2 grams, and Sugar: 1 grams.

GREEK YOGURT PARFAIT

Prep Time: 10 minutes
Total Time: 10 minutes
Servings: 4

Ingredients:

- 2 cups plain Greek yogurt
- 1 cup fresh berries (strawberries, blueberries, raspberries)
- 1/2 cup granola
- Optional: honey or maple syrup for drizzling

Directions:

1. In serving glasses or bowls, layer 1/4 cup of Greek yogurt at the bottom.
2. Place a generous layer of fresh berries on the surface of the yogurt.
3. If you prefer a sweeter taste, you have the option to drizzle honey or maple syrup over the top of the dish, providing an additional touch of sweetness.
4. Repeat the layers with another 1/4 cup of Greek yogurt, more berries, and granola.
5. If desired, enhance the sweetness by drizzling honey or maple syrup over the top.
6. Repeat the layering process for the remaining glasses or bowls.
7. Serve the Greek yogurt parfaits immediately or refrigerate until ready to serve.

Nutritional breakdown per serving:

Calories: 200 kcal, Protein: 18 grams, Carbohydrates: 25 grams, Fat: 4 grams, Saturated Fat: 1 grams, Cholesterol: 15 milligrams, Sodium: 80 milligrams, Fiber: 3 grams, and Sugar: 10 grams.

BRUSCHETTA

Prep Time: 15 minutes
Cooking Time: 5 minutes
Total Time: 20 minutes
Servings: 4

Ingredients:

- 4 slices of crusty bread (baguette or Italian bread)
- 2 ripe tomatoes, diced
- 1/4 cup fresh basil leaves, chopped
- 2 cloves garlic, minced
- 2 tablespoons extra-virgin olive oil
- 1 tablespoon balsamic vinegar
- Salt and pepper, to taste

Directions:

1. Preheat the broiler in your oven.
2. In a bowl, combine the diced tomatoes, chopped basil, minced garlic, olive oil, balsamic vinegar, salt, and pepper. Mix well to combine all the ingredients.
3. Position the bread slices on a baking sheet and transfer them to the broiler. Toast each side for about 2-3 minutes, or until they achieve a desired golden brown hue and a crispy texture.
4. Once the bread is toasted, carefully remove it from the oven and let it cool for a short while before handling.
5. Spoon the tomato and basil mixture onto each bread slice, spreading it evenly.
6. Present the bruschetta promptly, either as an appetizer or a light snack, for immediate enjoyment.

Nutritional breakdown per serving(1 serving, 1 slice of bruschetta):

Calories: 170 kcal, Protein: 4 grams, Carbohydrates: 20 grams, Fat: 8 grams, Saturated Fat: 1 grams, Cholesterol: 5 milligrams, Sodium: 200 milligrams, Fiber: 2 grams, and Sugar: 3 grams.

MINI STUFFED PEPPERS

Prep Time: 20 minutes

Cooking Time: 20 minutes

Total Time: 40 minutes

Servings: 4 (approximately 16 mini stuffed peppers)

Ingredients:

- 16 mini sweet peppers
- 1 cup cooked quinoa
- 1/2 cup of black beans, rinsed and drained
- 1/2 cup corn kernels
- 1/2 cup diced tomatoes
- 1/4 cup diced red onion
- 1/4 cup chopped fresh cilantro
- 1 tablespoon lime juice
- 1 teaspoon ground cumin
- 1/2 teaspoon chili powder
- Salt and pepper, to taste
- Optional toppings: shredded cheese, sour cream, avocado slices

Directions:

1. To ensure a successful cooking process, it is important to start by preheating the oven to 375°F (190°C).
2. To begin the preparation of the mini sweet peppers, carefully remove the tops and proceed to eliminate the seeds and membranes.
3. In a mixing bowl, combine the cooked quinoa, black beans, corn kernels, diced tomatoes, red onion, cilantro, lime juice, ground cumin, chili powder, salt, and pepper. Mix well to combine all the ingredients.
4. Spoon the quinoa mixture into each mini sweet pepper, filling them evenly.
5. Following the previous step, carefully arrange the stuffed peppers on a baking sheet and transfer them to the preheated oven. Allow them to bake for approximately 15-20 minutes, or until the peppers reach a tender consistency and the filling is thoroughly heated.
6. Once the designated cooking time has passed, gently take out the stuffed peppers from the oven and provide them with a short interval to cool down.
7. Serve the mini stuffed peppers warm, and if desired, top them with shredded cheese, sour cream, or avocado slices.

Nutritional breakdown per serving(1 serving, approximately 4 mini stuffed peppers):

Calories: 180 kcal, Protein: 8 grams, Carbohydrates: 36 grams, Fat: 2 grams, Saturated Fat: 0 grams, Cholesterol: 5 milligrams, Sodium: 150 milligrams, Fiber: 8 grams, and Sugar: 6 grams.

SMASHED AVOCADO TOAST

Prep Time: 5 minutes
Total Time: 5 minutes
Servings: 1

Ingredients:

- 1 small avocado
- 1 teaspoon fresh lemon juice
- 1/4 teaspoon Kosher salt
- 1/4 teaspoon freshly ground black pepper
- 1 slice whole grain bread, toasted
- 1 teaspoon extra-virgin olive oil
- Optional garnish: Maldon sea salt flakes or red pepper flakes

Directions:

1. In a small bowl, combine the avocado, lemon juice, salt, and pepper.
2. Utilizing the back of a fork, apply gentle pressure and mash the avocado until it reaches the consistency that suits your preference.
3. Spread the mashed avocado mixture evenly on the toasted bread.
4. Drizzle the olive oil over the avocado.
5. Sprinkle with desired garnish, such as Maldon sea salt flakes or red pepper flakes.
6. Serve the smashed avocado toast immediately.

Nutritional breakdown per serving:

Calories: 200 kcal, Protein: 5 grams, Carbohydrates: 18 grams, Fat: 13 grams, Saturated Fat: 2 grams, Cholesterol: 5 milligrams, Sodium: 295 milligrams, Fiber: 7 grams, and Sugar: 5 grams.

MINI PITA PIZZAS

Prep Time: 10 minutes
Cooking Time: 10 minutes
Total Time: 20 minutes
Servings: 4 (approximately 8 mini pita pizzas)

Ingredients:

- 4 mini pita bread rounds
- 1/2 cup pizza sauce
- 1 cup shredded mozzarella cheese
- Optional toppings: sliced pepperoni, diced bell peppers, sliced olives, sliced mushrooms, etc.
- Optional garnish: fresh basil leaves

Directions:

1. To ensure a successful cooking process, it is important to start by preheating the oven to 400°F (200°C).
2. Place the mini pita bread rounds on a baking sheet.
3. Take each pita bread round and evenly spread a thin layer of pizza sauce across its surface.
4. Generously sprinkle shredded mozzarella cheese over the sauce, ensuring an even distribution across the surface.
5. Place your desired toppings on top of the cheese, allowing you to customize your dish according to your preferences.
6. Once the oven is preheated, carefully place the baking sheet inside and bake for approximately 8-10 minutes. Keep an eye on it and remove from the oven when the cheese is melted and has started to bubble.
7. Remove the mini pita pizzas from the oven and let them cool slightly.
8. Garnish with fresh basil leaves, if desired.
9. Serve the mini pita pizzas warm as an appetizer or a light meal.

Nutritional breakdown per serving(1 serving, 2 mini pita pizzas):

Calories: 300 kcal, Protein: 12 grams, Carbohydrates: 40 grams, Fat: 10 grams, Saturated Fat: 5 grams, Cholesterol: 30 milligrams, Sodium: 500 milligrams, Fiber: 2 grams, and Sugar: 2 grams.

VEGGIE SPRING ROLLS

Prep Time: 20 minutes

Cooking Time: 10 minutes

Total Time: 30 minutes

Servings: 6 (approximately 12 spring rolls)

Ingredients:

- 14-oz (397-g) bag coleslaw mix or thinly sliced cabbage
- 1 red bell pepper, thinly sliced
- 1 cucumber, thinly sliced
- 1 cup (72 g) shredded iceberg lettuce
- 1 bunch fresh basil leaves (optional)
- 12 rice paper wraps
- Optional: 1 teaspoon Sriracha sauce
- Optional: 1 tablespoon hoisin sauce, thinned with water

Directions:

1. In a large bowl, combine the coleslaw, mix or thinly sliced cabbage, red bell pepper, cucumber, and shredded iceberg lettuce. Toss to mix the vegetables together.
2. Fill a pan large enough for the rice paper wraps to lie flat with 1 cup of very warm water.
3. To prepare the rice paper, submerge a single sheet in warm water for around 20 seconds. The goal is to achieve a pliable texture without it becoming overly soft.
4. Place the soaked rice paper wrap on a cutting board and gently flatten it.
5. Place a small amount of the vegetable mixture slightly below the center of the rice paper wrap.
6. If desired, drizzle Sriracha sauce over the vegetables for added spice.
7. Begin by folding the sides of the rice paper wrap over the filling. After that, tightly roll the rice paper up from the bottom, making sure to enclose the filling completely. By following these steps, you will achieve a well-wrapped and neatly presented rice paper roll.
8. Continue the process by repeating the same steps with the remaining rice paper wraps and vegetable mixture. This ensures consistency and allows for the creation of multiple rice paper wraps with the desired filling.
9. Serve the veggie spring rolls immediately with a dipping sauce of your choice, such as thinned hoisin sauce or soy sauce.

Nutritional breakdown per serving(1 serving, 2 spring rolls):

Calories: 120 kcal, Protein: 3 grams, Carbohydrates: 28 grams, Fat: 0.5 grams, Saturated Fat: 0 grams, Cholesterol: 5 milligrams, Sodium: 200 milligrams, Fiber: 3 grams, and Sugar: 4 grams.

SPINACH AND ARTICHOKE DIP

Prep Time: 10 minutes
Cooking Time: 20 minutes
Total Time: 30 minutes
Servings: 8

Ingredients:

- 8 oz (225 g) cream cheese, softened
- 1/2 cup sour cream
- 1/2 cup mayonnaise
- 1 cup grated Parmesan cheese
- 1 cup shredded mozzarella cheese
- 1 clove garlic, minced
- 1/2 teaspoon dried basil
- 1/2 teaspoon garlic salt
- 1/4 teaspoon salt
- 1/4 teaspoon black pepper
- 1 cup frozen chopped spinach, thawed and squeezed dry
- 1 cup canned artichoke hearts, drained and chopped

Directions:

1. To ensure a successful cooking process, it is important to start by preheating the oven to 350°F (175°C).
2. In a mixing bowl, combine the softened cream cheese, sour cream, mayonnaise, Parmesan cheese, mozzarella cheese, minced garlic, dried basil, garlic salt, salt, and black pepper. Ensure all the ingredients are thoroughly combined by mixing them well.
3. Stir the chopped spinach and artichoke hearts into the cream cheese mixture, ensuring that they are evenly distributed.
4. Move the mixture to a baking dish that is suitable for use in the oven, ensuring that it is spread out evenly.
5. Allow the dip to bake in the preheated oven for around 20 minutes, or until it reaches a hot and bubbly consistency.
6. Remove from the oven and let it cool for a few minutes before serving.
7. Serve the spinach and artichoke dip warm with tortilla chips, crackers, or bread.

Nutritional breakdown per serving:

Calories: 250 kcal, Protein: 7 grams, Carbohydrates: 4 grams, Fat: 23 grams, Saturated Fat: 10 grams, Cholesterol: 30 milligrams, Sodium: 520 milligrams, Fiber: 1 grams, and Sugar: 1 grams.

FRUIT KABOBS

Prep Time: 15 minutes

Total Time: 15 minutes

Servings: 6 (approximately 12 fruit kabobs)

Ingredients:

- 2 cups fresh strawberries
- 2 cups fresh pineapple chunks
- 2 cups fresh watermelon chunks
- 2 cups fresh grapes (any variety)
- 2 cups fresh blueberries
- 12 wooden or bamboo skewers

Directions:

1. Wash and prepare all the fruits. Hull and halve the strawberries. Cut the pineapple and watermelon into bite-sized chunks. After giving them a good rinse, separate the grapes from the stems.
2. Take a wooden or bamboo skewer and thread a strawberry, followed by a pineapple chunk, a watermelon chunk, a grape, and a blueberry. Continue repeating this pattern until the skewer is filled, ensuring to leave a small space at the end for convenient handling.
3. Repeat the process with the remaining skewers and fruits.
4. Serve the fruit kabobs immediately or refrigerate until ready to serve.

Nutritional breakdown per serving(1 serving, 2 fruit kabobs):

Calories: 100 kcal, Protein: 1 grams, Carbohydrates: 26 grams, Fat: 0 grams, Saturated Fat: 0 grams, Cholesterol: 0 milligrams, Sodium: 0 milligrams, Fiber: 4 grams, and Sugar: 19 grams.

STUFFED MUSHROOMS

Prep Time: 20 minutes
Cooking Time: 20 minutes
Total Time: 40 minutes
Servings: 12 (2 stuffed mushrooms per serving)

Ingredients:

- 24 large cremini or white button mushrooms (about 2 inches wide)
- 2 tablespoons olive oil, divided
- 1 small onion, finely chopped
- 3 cloves garlic, minced
- 1/2 cup panko breadcrumbs
- 1/2 cup freshly grated Parmesan cheese
- 1 tablespoon chopped fresh Italian parsley
- 1 teaspoon fresh thyme leaves
- 1 teaspoon lemon zest
- 1/2 teaspoon kosher salt
- Optional: Freshly ground black pepper, to taste

Directions:

1. To ensure a successful cooking process, it is important to start by preheating the oven to 375°F (190°C).
2. To clean the mushrooms, gently wipe them using a damp cloth or paper towel. Next, separate the stems and keep them aside.
3. To start, heat 1 tablespoon of olive oil in a large skillet over medium heat using a suitable cooking utensil. After the oil has reached the desired temperature, add the chopped onion and minced garlic to the skillet. Continue sautéing the mixture for about 3-4 minutes, or until the onion reaches a translucent state and the garlic releases its delightful aroma.
4. Take the reserved mushroom stems and finely chop them before adding them to the skillet. Cook for an additional 3-4 minutes, until the mushroom stems are tender.
5. After removing the skillet from the heat, proceed to transfer the mixture from the skillet to a mixing bowl with caution.
6. To the bowl, add the panko breadcrumbs, grated Parmesan cheese, chopped parsley, fresh thyme leaves, lemon zest, salt, and optional black pepper. Mix well to combine all the ingredients.
7. Evenly distribute the remaining 1 tablespoon of olive oil by drizzling it over a baking sheet.

8. Take each mushroom cap and fill it generously with the breadcrumb mixture, pressing it down slightly.
9. Position the stuffed mushrooms on the baking sheet that has been prepared, ensuring they are arranged in a single layer.
10. Once the stuffed mushrooms are positioned on the baking sheet, carefully place it in the preheated oven. Allow the mushrooms to bake for about 15-20 minutes until they reach a tender consistency and their tops develop a pleasing golden brown hue.
11. Remove from the oven and let them cool for a few minutes before serving.
12. Serve the stuffed mushrooms warm as an appetizer or side dish.

Nutritional breakdown per serving(1 serving, 2 stuffed mushrooms):

Calories: 90 kcal, Protein: 4 grams, Carbohydrates: 7 grams, Fat: 5 grams, Saturated Fat: 1 grams, Cholesterol: 40 milligrams, Sodium: 200 milligrams, Fiber: 1 grams, and Sugar: 1 grams.

SALSA AND GUACAMOLE DUO

Prep Time: 15 minutes

Total Time: 15 minutes

Servings: 6 (approximately 2 tablespoons of each salsa and guacamole per serving)

Ingredients for Salsa:

- 2 ripe tomatoes, diced
- 1/2 red onion, finely chopped
- 1 jalapeno pepper, seeds removed and finely chopped
- 1/4 cup chopped fresh cilantro
- 1 clove garlic, minced
- Juice of 1 lime
- Salt and pepper to taste

Ingredients for Guacamole:

- 3 ripe avocados
- 1/4 cup diced red onion
- 1/4 cup chopped fresh cilantro
- Juice of 1 lime
- 1/2 teaspoon salt
- Optional: 1/2 teaspoon cumin powder

Directions:

1. In a mixing bowl, combine all the ingredients for the salsa - diced tomatoes, chopped red onion, jalapeno pepper, chopped cilantro, minced garlic, lime juice, salt, and pepper. Mix well to combine.
2. After tasting the mixture, make any necessary adjustments to the seasoning based on your personal preferences. Once you are satisfied with the flavor, set the seasoned mixture aside for later use.
3. Take a separate bowl and use a fork to scoop out the flesh of the avocados. Proceed to mash the avocados with the fork until you reach the desired consistency.
4. Add the diced red onion, chopped cilantro, lime juice, salt, and optional cumin powder to the mashed avocados. Mix well to combine.
5. Taste and adjust the seasoning if needed.
6. Serve the salsa and guacamole together in separate bowls.
7. Savor the combination of salsa and guacamole by serving it alongside tortilla chips or as a delectable topping for tacos, burritos, or grilled meats.

Nutritional breakdown per serving(1 serving, approximately 2 tablespoons of each salsa and guacamole):

Calories: 80 kcal, Protein: 1 grams, Carbohydrates: 6 grams, Fat: 7 grams, Saturated Fat: 1 grams, Cholesterol: 5 milligrams, Sodium: 200 milligrams, Fiber: 4 grams, and Sugar: 1 grams.

CHOCOLATE-DIPPED STRAWBERRIES

Prep Time: 10 minutes
Cooking Time: 5 minutes
Total Time: 15 minutes
Servings: 24 strawberries

Ingredients:

- 24 fresh strawberries
- 2 cups semisweet chocolate chips
- 2 tablespoons coconut oil

Directions:

1. In readiness for usage, cover a large baking sheet with parchment paper.
2. Once the strawberries have been thoroughly rinsed, carefully dry them by gently patting them with paper towels.
3. In a microwave-safe bowl, mix together the semisweet chocolate chips and coconut oil, ensuring that the bowl is suitable for use in the microwave.
4. Microwave the chocolate mixture in 30-second intervals, stirring in between, until completely melted and smooth.
5. Gently hold the strawberry by its stem and submerge it into the melted chocolate, ensuring that all sides are coated evenly. Shake off any excess chocolate before proceeding with the next step.
6. Place the chocolate-covered strawberry on the prepared baking sheet. Repeat with the remaining strawberries, spacing them so they don't touch.
7. Refrigerate the strawberries for about 20 minutes to set the chocolate.
8. Remove the strawberries from the refrigerator and let them harden completely at room temperature.
9. Serve the chocolate-dipped strawberries the same day, if possible.

Nutritional breakdown per serving(1 serving, 1 chocolate-dipped strawberry):

Calories: 80 kcal, Protein: 1 grams, Carbohydrates: 9 grams, Fat: 5 grams, Saturated Fat: 3 grams, Cholesterol: 30 milligrams, Sodium: 8 milligrams, Fiber: 1 grams, and Sugar: 8 grams.

CHAPTER 7
DESSERTS
RECIPES

MINI BERRY TARTS

Prep Time: 20 minutes
Cooking Time: 12 minutes
Total Time: 32 minutes
Servings: 24 mini tarts

Ingredients:

- 1 package (16.5 oz) of refrigerated sugar cookie dough
- 1 package (3.4 oz) of instant vanilla pudding mix
- 1 1/2 cups cold milk
- 1 cup Cool Whip (thawed)
- Fresh berries (strawberries, blueberries, raspberries) for topping

Directions:

1. Before you proceed to the next step, take a moment to verify that the oven has indeed been preheated to 350°F (175°C).
2. To prevent sticking, lightly grease a mini muffin tin using non-stick cooking spray.
3. Using small portions of the sugar cookie dough, carefully press them into the bottom and up the sides of each muffin cup, shaping them into tart shell forms.
4. Place the tart shells in the preheated oven and bake them for approximately 10-12 minutes, or until they turn a beautiful golden brown color.
5. After baking, carefully remove the tart shells from the oven and let them cool completely while still inside the muffin tin.
6. In a mixing bowl, adhere to the instructions on the package to properly combine the instant vanilla pudding mix and cold milk. Be sure to mix them together thoroughly until the mixture is well combined.
7. Once the pudding has set, fold in the Cool Whip until well combined.
8. Spoon the vanilla pudding mixture into the cooled tart shells, filling them almost to the top.
9. Top each tart with fresh berries of your choice.
10. Refrigerate the mini berry tarts for at least 1 hour before serving.
11. Serve chilled and enjoy!

Nutritional breakdown per serving(1 mini tart):

Calories: 110 kcal, Protein: 1 grams, Carbohydrates: 17 grams, Fat: 4 grams, Saturated Fat: 1 grams, Cholesterol: 20 milligrams, Sodium: 125 milligrams, Fiber: 0 grams, and Sugar: 10 grams.

CHOCOLATE MUG CAKE

Prep Time: 5 minutes
Cooking Time: 2 minutes
Total Time: 7 minutes
Servings: 1

Ingredients:

- 4 tablespoons all-purpose flour
- 2 tablespoons granulated sugar
- 2 tablespoons unsweetened cocoa powder
- 1/8 teaspoon baking powder
- Pinch of salt
- 3 tablespoons milk
- 2 tablespoons vegetable oil
- 1/4 teaspoon vanilla extract
- Optional: Chocolate chips or nuts for topping

Directions:

1. Whisk the all-purpose flour, granulated sugar, cocoa powder, baking powder, and salt together in a microwave-safe mug until they are well combined and fully incorporated.
2. In the mug, combine the milk, vegetable oil, and vanilla extract. Stir the mixture vigorously until a smooth batter forms, ensuring there are no lumps remaining.
3. If desired, sprinkle some chocolate chips or nuts on top of the batter.
4. Put the mug in the microwave and cook it on high power for approximately 1 minute and 30 seconds to 2 minutes. Keep an eye on the cake as cooking times may differ depending on your microwave's wattage. The cake should rise and set in the center when it is done.
5. After heating, exercise caution while taking the mug out of the microwave as it will be hot. After removing the cake from the microwave, it is recommended to let it cool for a minute or two before handling it.
6. Enjoy the delightful warmth of the chocolate mug cake, either by savoring it directly from the mug or transferring it onto a plate. For an added touch of indulgence, you can enhance the experience by adding a dollop of whipped cream or a scoop of ice cream on top.

Nutritional breakdown per serving:

Calories: 380 kcal, Protein: 6 grams, Carbohydrates: 48 grams, Fat: 20 grams, Saturated Fat: 3grams, Cholesterol: 0 milligrams, Sodium: 220 milligrams, Fiber: 4 grams, and Sugar: 26 grams.

INDIVIDUAL FRUIT CRUMBLES

Prep Time: 15 minutes
Cooking Time: 25 minutes
Total Time: 40 minutes
Servings: 4 individual fruit crumbles

Ingredients:

- 2 cups mixed fresh berries
- 2 tablespoons granulated sugar
- 1 tablespoon cornstarch
- 1/2 teaspoon vanilla extract

For the Crumble Topping:

- 1/2 cup all-purpose flour
- 1/4 cup rolled oats
- 1/4 cup packed brown sugar
- 1/4 teaspoon ground cinnamon
- 1/4 cup of chilled unsalted butter, cut into small pieces

Optional:

- Add a finishing touch with vanilla ice cream or whipped cream

Directions:

1. Before you proceed to the next step, take a moment to verify that the oven has indeed been preheated to 375°F (190°C).
2. In a mixing bowl, combine the mixed fresh berries, granulated sugar, cornstarch, and vanilla extract. Toss gently until the berries are coated evenly. Set aside.
3. To make the irresistible crumble topping, simply gather a separate bowl and combine the all-purpose flour, rolled oats, brown sugar, and ground cinnamon. Taking care to thoroughly mix all the ingredients together will result in a well-incorporated and flavorful crumble topping that will elevate your dish.
4. Next, incorporate the cold unsalted butter pieces into the crumble mixture. To create a coarse crumb-like texture, you can use either your fingertips or a pastry cutter to cut the butter into the dry ingredients.
5. Divide the berry mixture evenly among four individual ramekins or oven-safe dishes.
6. Sprinkle the crumble topping over the berries, covering them completely.

7. After arranging the ramekins on a baking sheet, carefully transfer them to the preheated oven. Let them bake for approximately 20-25 minutes until the fruit starts bubbling and the crumble topping turns a beautiful golden brown.
8. Remove from the oven and let the individual fruit crumbles cool for a few minutes.
9. Serve the fruit crumbles warm, optionally topped with vanilla ice cream or whipped cream.

Nutritional breakdown per serving:

Calories: 250 kcal, Protein: 3 grams, Carbohydrates: 40 grams, Fat: 10 grams, Saturated Fat: 6 grams, Cholesterol: 25 milligrams, Sodium: 5 milligrams, Fiber: 4 grams, and Sugar: 20 grams.

VEGAN BANANA SPLIT

Prep Time: 10 minutes
Total Time: 10 minutes
Servings: 1

Ingredients:

- 1 ripe banana
- 1/4 cup dairy-free vanilla ice cream
- 2 tablespoons dairy-free chocolate sauce
- 2 tablespoons chopped nuts
- 2 tablespoons fresh berries (such as strawberries or blueberries)
- Optional toppings: dairy-free whipped cream, shredded coconut, sprinkles

Directions:

1. Peel the ripe banana and slice it in half lengthwise.
2. Place the banana halves in a serving dish or bowl.
3. Scoop the dairy-free vanilla ice cream on top of the banana halves.
4. Drizzle the dairy-free chocolate sauce over the ice cream.
5. Sprinkle the chopped nuts and fresh berries on top.
6. For additional flavor and customization, feel free to add any optional toppings you desire. Some popular choices include dairy-free whipped cream, shredded coconut, or sprinkles.
7. Serve the vegan banana split immediately and enjoy!

Nutritional breakdown per serving:

Calories: 300 kcal, Protein: 4 grams, Carbohydrates: 40 grams, Fat: 15 grams, Saturated Fat: 3 grams, Cholesterol: 0 milligrams, Sodium: 50 milligrams, Fiber: 6 grams, and Sugar: 20 grams.

MINI APPLE PIES

Prep Time: 30 minutes
Cooking Time: 20 minutes
Total Time: 50 minutes
Servings: 6 mini apple pies

Ingredients:

- 2 medium-sized apples (such as Honeycrisp or Granny Smith)
- 2 tablespoons granulated sugar
- 1 tablespoon all-purpose flour
- 1/2 teaspoon ground cinnamon
- 1/4 teaspoon ground nutmeg
- 1 package refrigerated pie crusts (2 crusts)
- 1 tablespoon non-dairy milk (such as almond or soy milk)
- Optional: powdered sugar for dusting

Directions:

1. For optimal baking results, begin by preheating your oven to 375°F (190°C). This will ensure that your baking surface is ready and your food will cook evenly.
2. To prepare the apples, start by peeling them. Next, remove the cores and dice them into small pieces.
3. To create the apple mixture, gather a mixing bowl and combine the diced apples, granulated sugar, all-purpose flour, ground cinnamon, and ground nutmeg. To ensure even coating of the mixture, toss the ingredients together until the apples are thoroughly coated.
4. Roll out the refrigerated pie crusts on a lightly floured surface. To create the pie crusts, you can use a round cookie cutter or a glass to cut out circles that are slightly larger than the openings of your mini pie pans.
5. Press the pie crust circles into the mini pie pans, making sure to cover the bottom and sides.
6. To ensure that each mini pie is filled with the apple mixture, distribute the mixture evenly among the pans, making sure to fill each pie crust completely.
7. To add a decorative touch to each mini pie, roll out the remaining pie crust and cut it into thin strips. Then, create a lattice pattern on top of each pie by weaving the strips over and under each other.
8. To achieve a delightful golden color when the pies are baked, take a moment before placing them in the oven to brush the tops with non-dairy milk. This simple step will enhance their appearance and add to the overall appeal of the final result.

9. Begin by arranging the mini apple pies onto the baking sheet that has been prepared. Place them in the preheated oven and allow them to bake for approximately 18-20 minutes. Keep a close eye on them until the crust reaches a beautiful golden brown color, and the filling starts to bubble enticingly.
10. Once the pies are done baking, carefully take them out of the oven and place them on a wire rack to cool. Allowing them to cool on the rack will help to prevent them from becoming soggy, as it allows air to circulate around the pies.
11. Once cooled, dust the tops of the mini apple pies with powdered sugar, if desired.
12. Serve the mini apple pies warm or at room temperature.

Nutritional breakdown per serving(1 mini apple pie):

Calories: 220 kcal, Protein: 2 grams, Carbohydrates: 31 grams, Fat: 10 grams, Saturated Fat: 4 grams, Cholesterol: 0 milligrams, Sodium: 160 milligrams, Fiber: 2 grams, and Sugar: 12 grams.

CHOCOLATE-DIPPED COCONUT MACAROONS

Prep Time: 20 minutes
Cooking Time: 20 minutes
Total Time: 40 minutes
Servings: 24 macaroons

Ingredients:

- 1 cup sweetened condensed milk
- 1/2 teaspoon almond extract
- 1 1/2 teaspoons vanilla extract
- 1/4 teaspoon fine salt
- 1 large egg white
- 3 cups shredded unsweetened coconut
- 4 ounces semisweet chocolate, chopped (or to taste)

Directions:

1. To achieve optimal results, begin by preheating your oven to 350°F (175°C). In preparation for the following step, grab a baking sheet and apply a layer of parchment paper to it.
2. To create the mixture, gather a mixing bowl and combine the sweetened condensed milk, almond extract, vanilla extract, salt, and egg white. Utilize a whisk to blend the ingredients until they are fully incorporated.
3. Incorporate approximately 2 1/3 cups of shredded coconut into the mixture, ensuring it is evenly distributed. Carefully blend the ingredients using a spatula until they reach a sticky and cohesive consistency.
4. Shape the mixture into balls either by using a sorbet scoop or by using your hands. Afterward, coat the balls with the remaining shredded coconut by rolling them in it.
5. Arrange the macaroons evenly on the baking sheet that has been prepared.
6. Give the macaroons enough time to bake in the preheated oven, usually around 20 minutes, until they reach the desired golden color.
7. Let the macaroons cool to room temperature, at least 20 minutes.
8. Take a microwave-safe bowl and melt the chopped semisweet chocolate in it. For a smooth and melted consistency, microwave the chocolate in intervals of 30 seconds, ensuring to stir in between each interval until it is completely melted.
9. Immerse the bottom of each macaroon into the melted chocolate, ensuring that it reaches a depth of approximately 1/4 inch (6 mm). Place them, chocolate side down, on the parchment-lined baking sheet.
10. Refrigerate the macaroons until the chocolate is firm, about 1 hour.

11. Serve the chocolate-dipped coconut macaroons and enjoy!

Nutritional breakdown per serving(1 macaroon):

Calories: 133 kcal, Protein: 2 grams, Carbohydrates: 15 grams, Fat: 8 grams, Saturated Fat: 7 grams, Cholesterol: 3 milligrams, Sodium: 51 milligrams, Fiber: 2 grams, and Sugar: 13 grams.

INDIVIDUAL CHOCOLATE PUDDING CUPS

Prep Time: 5 minutes
Cook Time: 5 minutes
Total Time: 1 hour and 10 minutes
Servings: 4

Ingredients:

- 1/2 cup granulated sugar
- 1/3 cup unsweetened cocoa powder
- 1/4 cup cornstarch
- 1/4 teaspoon kosher salt
- 2 1/4 cups milk
- 1 1/2 teaspoons vanilla extract
- 2 tablespoons butter, room temperature
- Optional toppings: whipped cream, chocolate shavings, fresh berries

Directions:

1. To create a homogeneous mixture, start by placing a medium saucepan on the stove. Then, add granulated sugar, cocoa powder, cornstarch, and salt to the saucepan. Stir the ingredients together using a whisk until they are thoroughly combined.
2. Ensure proper integration by slowly pouring the milk into the saucepan while whisking continuously.
3. To initiate the process, position the saucepan on the stove and set the heat to medium. Continuously stir the mixture while applying heat until it reaches a boiling point. Let it cook for an extra minute until it thickens to the desired consistency.
4. Take the saucepan off the heat and blend in the vanilla extract and butter until they are fully melted and incorporated.
5. Pour the chocolate pudding into individual serving cups or ramekins.
6. To avoid the formation of a skin, ensure that each cup has a layer of plastic wrap placed directly on its surface, ensuring full contact.
7. Refrigerate the pudding cups for at least 1 hour to chill and set.
8. Once chilled, remove the plastic wrap and garnish the individual chocolate pudding cups with whipped cream, chocolate shavings, or fresh berries, if desired.
9. Serve the chocolate pudding cups chilled and enjoy!

Nutritional breakdown per serving(1 pudding cup):

Calories: 230 kcal, Protein: 5 grams, Carbohydrates: 38 grams, Fat: 8 grams, Saturated Fat: 5 grams, Cholesterol: 20 milligrams, Sodium: 160 milligrams, Fiber: 2 grams, and Sugar: 26 grams.

BERRY PARFAIT

Prep Time: 15 minutes

Total Time: 1 hour and 15 minutes

Servings: 4

Ingredients:

- 2 cups mixed berries
- 2 tablespoons granulated sugar
- 1 cup non-dairy yogurt (such as coconut or almond yogurt)
- 1/2 cup granola
- Optional toppings: fresh mint leaves, additional berries

Directions:

1. In a bowl, combine the mixed berries and granulated sugar. Toss gently until the berries are coated in sugar. Let them sit for about 10 minutes to release their juices.
2. In serving glasses or bowls, layer the berry mixture, non-dairy yogurt, and granola. Continue adding layers until the glasses are filled to the brim.
3. Top each parfait with additional berries and fresh mint leaves, if desired.
4. To achieve the desired coolness and enhance the flavors, refrigerate the parfait for at least 1 hour after covering it with plastic wrap.
5. Serve the berry parfaits chilled and enjoy!

Nutritional breakdown per serving(1 parfait):

Calories: 180 kcal, Protein: 4 grams, Carbohydrates: 34 grams, Fat: 4 grams, Saturated Fat: 1 grams, Cholesterol: 0 milligrams, Sodium: 40 milligrams, Fiber: 5 grams, and Sugar: 19 grams.

MINI CHEESECAKES

Prep Time: 20 minutes
Total Time: 2 hours and 20 minutes
Servings: 12 mini cheesecakes

Ingredients:

- 1 cup graham cracker crumbs
- 2 tablespoons granulated sugar
- 4 tablespoons unsalted butter, melted
- 16 ounces cream cheese, softened
- 1/2 cup granulated sugar
- 2 large eggs
- 1 teaspoon vanilla extract
- Optional toppings: fruit preserves, chocolate ganache, whipped cream

Directions:

1. To get started, ensure that the oven is preheated to 325°F (160°C). Then, prepare the muffin tin by lining it with paper liners.
2. In a bowl, combine the graham cracker crumbs, granulated sugar, and melted butter. Mix until the crumbs are evenly coated.
3. Divide the crumb mixture evenly among the paper liners, pressing it down firmly to create the crust.
4. In a separate bowl, thoroughly combine the cream cheese and granulated sugar until a smooth and creamy mixture is achieved.
5. Add the eggs to the mixture one at a time, ensuring they are well incorporated before adding the next one. After adding the eggs, stir in the vanilla extract.
6. Ensure an even distribution of the cream cheese mixture over the crusts by using a spoon, taking care to fill each liner to around 3/4 of its capacity.
7. Place the prepared mixture in the preheated oven and bake for approximately 15-18 minutes, or until the edges are firm and the centers have a slight jiggle.
8. After baking, take the mini cheesecakes out of the oven and allow them to cool for a duration of 10 minutes while still in the muffin tin.
9. Move the mini cheesecakes to a wire rack, allowing them to cool completely. Once cooled, transfer them to the refrigerator and refrigerate for a minimum of 2 hours to achieve the desired chill and set.
10. Once chilled, remove the paper liners from the mini cheesecakes.
11. Top each mini cheesecake with your choice of fruit preserves, chocolate ganache, or whipped cream, if desired.

12. Serve the mini cheesecakes chilled and enjoy!

Nutritional breakdown per serving(1 mini cheesecake):

Calories: 250 kcal, Protein: 4 grams, Carbohydrates: 17 grams, Fat: 19 grams, Saturated Fat: 11 grams, Cholesterol: 85 milligrams, Sodium: 180 milligrams, Fiber: 0 grams, and Sugar: 13 grams.

GRILLED PINEAPPLE WITH COCONUT WHIPPED CREAM

Prep Time: 10 minutes

Cook Time: 6 minutes

Total Time: 1 hour and 16 minutes

Servings: 4

Ingredients:

- 1 ripe pineapple, peeled and cored
- 1 tablespoon honey
- 1 cup coconut cream, chilled overnight
- 1 tablespoon powdered sugar
- 1/2 teaspoon vanilla extract
- Optional toppings: shredded coconut, fresh mint leaves

Directions:

1. Preheat the grill to medium-high heat.
2. Slice the pineapple into 1/2-inch thick rounds.
3. Brush each pineapple slice with honey on both sides.
4. Position the pineapple slices onto the preheated grill and cook for approximately 3 minutes per side, or until distinctive grill marks materialize and the pineapple achieves a slight caramelized appearance.
5. Remove the grilled pineapple slices from the grill and let them cool to room temperature.
6. In a mixing bowl, blend together the chilled coconut cream, powdered sugar, and vanilla extract. Utilize an electric mixer to whip the mixture until it reaches the consistency of soft peaks.
7. After covering the bowl with plastic wrap, place it in the refrigerator for a minimum of 1 hour to allow the coconut whipped cream to cool and set.
8. To serve, place a grilled pineapple slice on a plate and top it with a dollop of coconut whipped cream.
9. If desired, add a garnish of shredded coconut and fresh mint leaves to enhance the presentation.
10. Repeat with the remaining pineapple slices and coconut whipped cream.
11. Serve the grilled pineapple with coconut whipped cream and enjoy!

Nutritional breakdown per serving:

Calories: 210 kcal, Protein: 1 grams, Carbohydrates: 23 grams, Fat: 14 grams, Saturated Fat: 12 grams, Cholesterol: 0 milligrams, Sodium: 5 milligrams, Fiber: 2 grams, and Sugar: 17 grams.

CHOCOLATE-DIPPED STRAWBERRIES

Prep Time: 15 minutes

Total Time: 35 minutes

Servings: 25 strawberries

Ingredients:

- 1 pint strawberries
- 2 cups semisweet chocolate chips
- 2 tablespoons coconut oil

Directions:

1. To commence the process, it is important to have a sizable baking sheet at the ready. This can be achieved by carefully lining the sheet with parchment paper. Proceed by rinsing the strawberries and gently drying them using paper towels.
2. To initiate the melting process, take a small microwave-safe bowl and combine the semisweet chocolate chips with coconut oil. Proceed by microwaving the mixture in 30-second intervals, pausing to stir in between each interval, until the chocolate achieves a thoroughly melted and smooth consistency.
3. To coat the strawberry with the melted chocolate, hold it by the stem and gently swirl it in the chocolate, making sure to cover all sides. Allow any excess chocolate to drip off.
4. Place the chocolate-dipped strawberry on the parchment-lined baking sheet. Repeat with the remaining strawberries, spacing them so they don't touch.
5. Once a duration of 20 minutes has elapsed, take out the strawberries from the refrigerator and allow them to fully harden at room temperature.
6. After a duration of 20 minutes, it is advised to remove the strawberries from the refrigerator and let them reach a complete hardening state at room temperature.
7. Serve the chocolate-dipped strawberries the same day, if possible, for the best taste and texture.

Nutritional breakdown per serving (1 strawberry):

Calories: 80 kcal, Protein: 1 grams, Carbohydrates: 9 grams, Fat: 5 grams, Saturated Fat: 3 grams, Cholesterol: 0 milligrams, Sodium: 2 milligrams, Fiber: 1 grams, and Sugar: 8 grams.

CHIA SEED PUDDING

Prep Time: 5 minutes

Total Time: 2 hours and 5 minutes

Servings: 2

Ingredients:

- 1 cup of milk (almond or preferred)
- 1/4 cup chia seeds
- 1 tablespoon of sweetener (maple syrup, honey, or agave nectar)
- 1 teaspoon pure vanilla extract (optional)
- Pinch of kosher salt
- Optional toppings: sliced fruit, granola, jam, nuts

Directions:

1. In a medium bowl, combine the almond milk (or milk of your choice), chia seeds, sweetener (maple syrup, honey, or agave nectar), vanilla extract (optional), and a pinch of kosher salt.
2. Stir the mixture together until well combined.
3. Seal the bowl with a lid or cover it with plastic wrap.
4. To achieve a pudding-like consistency, it is recommended to chill the bowl in the refrigerator for at least 2 hours. However, for optimal results, it is best to leave it overnight, allowing the chia seeds to fully absorb the liquid.
5. Once the chilling time is complete, it is important to thoroughly stir the chia pudding. Ensuring a smooth and consistent texture is crucial, and one way to achieve this is by breaking up any clumps.
6. Serve the chia pudding in individual bowls or jars.
7. Top with your choice of sliced fruit, granola, jam, nuts, or any other desired toppings.
8. Enjoy the chia seed pudding immediately or refrigerate for later consumption.

Nutritional breakdown per serving:

Calories: 189 kcal, Protein: 5 grams, Carbohydrates: 23 grams, Fat: 9 grams, Saturated Fat: 1 grams, Cholesterol: 0 milligrams, Sodium: 62 milligrams, Fiber: 10 grams, and Sugar: 9 grams.

CONCLUSION

In summary, the "Cookbook for Two" goes beyond being a mere compilation of recipes. rewrite down the text without plagiarism

It stands as a tribute to the profound influence of shared moments and the art of bonding through the marvels of culinary pleasures. It commemorates love, closeness, and the sheer delight of crafting meals that nurture not only the body but also the soul.

With each recipe and every turn of the page, this cookbook beckons you to embark on a gastronomic journey alongside your significant other, kindling a flame that goes beyond the mere act of preparing meals. It encourages you to explore new flavors, experiment with ingredients, and embrace the beauty of simplicity in your kitchen.

As you journey through the pages of the "Cookbook for Two," you will discover the magic that happens when two hearts and two sets of hands come together to create something extraordinary. The recipes within these pages will not only fill your plates but also create lasting memories and deepen the bond you share.

Whether you find delight in a comforting morning meal in bed, orchestrate an intimate candlelit dinner to commemorate a special occasion, or simply revel in the simple pleasures of cooking side by side, this culinary guide will serve as your unwavering beacon. It will empower you to express your love through food and inspire you to explore the endless possibilities that lie within your kitchen.

So, as you close this cookbook, remember that the journey does not end here. Allow the recipes and techniques you have uncovered to serve as the cornerstone for a lifetime filled with remarkable culinary explorations. Embrace the joy of cooking for two, relish in the flavors that dance on your palate, and cherish the moments of togetherness that each meal brings.

Thank you for embarking on this culinary voyage with us. May the "Cookbook for Two" continue to be a source of inspiration, connection, and delicious moments shared with your loved one. Bon appétit!

Made in the USA
Las Vegas, NV
20 June 2024

91263648R00103